MW00509082

Graphic layout, designer & art consultant
Fabio Riccobono

# THE GREAT POULTRY COOKBOOK

**TASTY RECIPES FOR GRILLED CHICKEN AND TURKEY
LOVERS TO COOK WITH THE WOOD PELLET GRILL.**

**MAT RAICHLEN**

# TABLE
# OF CONTENTS

# INTRODUCTION

# WHAT IS A PELLET SMOKER AND GRILL?

To provide you with a clear answer about the Wood Pellet Smoker and Grill, let us start by defining this grilling appliance. In fact, Pellet Smoker and Grills can be defined as an electric outdoor Smoker and Grill that is only fueled by wood pellets. Wood Pellet is a type of fuel that is characterized by its capsule size and is praised for its ability to enhance more flavors and tastes to the chosen smoked meat. And what is unique and special about wood pellet as a fuel is that it can grill, smoke, roast, braise and even bake according to its easy to follow instructions. I equipped with a control board that allows you to automatically maintain your desired temperature for several hours

# WHY CHOOSE TO USE A WOOD PELLET SMOKER AND GRILL?

Accurate, Pellet Smoker and Grills make an explosive mixture of sublime tastes and incredible deliciousness; it is a great Smoker and Grill appliance that you can use if you want to enjoy the taste of charcoal grill and at the same time you don't want to give up on the traditional taste of ovens. And what is more interesting about pellet Smoker and Grills is that, with a single button, you can grill, roast, bake, braise and smoke, your favorite meat portions.

# HOW TO USE A WOOD PELLET SMOKER AND GRILL?

Pellet Smoker and Grills function based on advanced digital technology and many mechanical parts. The pellet Smoker and Grill are then lit while the temperature is usually programmed with the help of a digital control board. Pellet Smoker and Grills work by using an algorithm so that it allows calculating the exact number of pellets you should use to reach the perfect temperature. Every Wood Pellet Grill is equipped with a rotating auger that allows to automatically feed the fire right from the hopper to the fire to maintain the same temperature. And even as the food continues cooking, the wood pellet Smoker and Grill will continue to drop the exact number of pellets needed to keep the perfect cooking temperature. But what can we cook with a pellet Smoker and Grill?

# WHAT DISHES CAN WE PREPARE ON A WOOD PELLET SMOKER AND GRILL?

Thanks to its versatile properties to smoke, grill, braise and kitchen oven, Wood Pellet Smoker and Grill can be used to cook endless dishes and recipes. In fact, there is no actual limit to the recipes you can cook like hot dogs, chicken, vegetables, seafood, rabbit,

ken, brisket, turkey and even more. The cooking
ess is very easy; all you have to do is to pack your
ite wood pellets into the hopper; then program
emperature you desire on the controller; then
e the food on the pellet Smoker and Grill. That is,
d the pellet will be able to maintain the tempera-
and keep the pellets burning.

t Smoker and Grills are characterized by being
ric and it requires a usual standard outlet of
it 110v so that you can power the digital board,
and auger.

e is a wide variety of types of pellet smokers and
like electric pellet smokers, wood fired grills,

wood pellet grills and wood pellet smokers; to name
a few pellet Smoker and Grill names. But all these
names refer to the same outdoor cooker appliance
that is only fueled by hardwood pellets. And there are
many brands of Wood Pellet Smoker and Grills, like
Traeger.

For instance, Traeger is known for being one of the
world's most well-known brands of pellet grills. Indeed,
Joe Traeger was the person who invented the pellet
grill during the mid-1980s, and he gave his name to
this invention. And when the Traeger patent expired,
many other Pellet Smoker and Grills came to life into
the market.

# MY SHOPPING
# TIPS!

# PELLET GRILLS

Traeger Pellet Grills: https://amzn.to/3rC8wX6

Traeger Grills Ranger Grill: https://amzn.to/3tJhi7x

# ACCESSORIES

Traeger Pellet Grill Cover:  https://amzn.to/3aGg0Bu

Traeger Pellet Sensor: https://amzn.to/2MOskYD

Traeger Pellet Folding Shelf: https://amzn.to/3cWALvM

Cooking Gloves: https://amzn.to/3aTDzXY

The Original Turkey Injector: https://amzn.to/3q5b0x0

Set of 5 Disposable Aluminum Wood-Fired Cooking: https://amzn.to/3tFz77E

# WOOD PELLETS

Traeger Grills PEL331 Signature Blend Grill: https://amzn.to/2YWogYM

Green Mountain Grills Premium Apple: https://amzn.to/2YZdQHU

# Chapter 1.

# THE FUNDAMENTALS OF SMOKING

# WHAT IS WOOD PELLET SMOKERS GRILL?

A pellet grill is essentially a multi-functional grill that has been so designed that the compressed wood pellets end up being the real source of fuel. They are outdoor cookers and tend to combine the different striking elements of smokers, gas grills, ovens, and even charcoal. The very reason which has cemented their popularity for ages have to be the kind of quality and flavor that they tend to infuse in the food you make on them.

Not only this, by varying the kind of wood pellet you are using, but you can also bring in the variation in the actual flavor of the food as well. Often, the best chefs use a mix and match technique of wood pellets to infuse the food with their signature flavor that have people hooked to their cooking in no time.

The clinical definition of a wood pellet smoker grill is smoking, grilling, roasting, and baking barbecue using compressed hardwood sawdust such as apple, cherry, hickory, maple, mesquite, oak, and other wood pellets. It is a pit. Wood pellet smoker grills provide the flavor profile and moisture that only hardwood dishes can achieve. Depending on the manufacturer and model, the grill temperature on many models can be well over 150 ° F to 600 ° F. Gone are the days when people say they cannot bake on wood pellet smoking grills!

Wood pellet smoker grills offer the succulence, convenience, and safety not found in charcoal or gas grills. The smoke here is not as thick as other smokers common to you. Its design provides the versatility and benefits of a convection oven. A wood pellet smoker grill is safe and easy to operate.

# HOW DO THEY WORK?

The grill would run on electricity and therefore it needs to be plugged in for the sake of deriving power.

The design is such that pellets have to be added to the hopper that in turn will funnel down owing to the presence of a rotating auger and a motor.

The auger aims to make sure that the pellets get pushed down to the fire pot at the pre-configured speed which is determined by the yard control panel showing the temperature. As soon as the pellets reach the fire pot, there is an ignition rod that creates a flame that in turn causes the production of smoke.

Also, a fan is present at the bottom which helps in pushing both the generated heat and smoke upwards on the grill and thereby allows for the convection style of even cooking.

This happens to be the basic mechanism of the working of a wood pellet grill. Knowing the different parts of the wood pellet grill and also the working mechanism will prepare you in a much better way to ensure that you can use the grill in the right manner.

However, before we venture further into the recipes, we are going to shift our focus on some important points about these grills. This is because the right knowledge is crucial to ensuring that you know what you are getting into.

# HOW TO PICK THE BEST WOOD PELLETS

What makes a wood pellet smoker and grill unique is the very thing that fuels it -- wood pellets. Wood pellets are compressed sawdust, made from either pine wood, birch wood, fir wood, or crop stalks. Culinary-wise, wood pellets are used mostly as fuel for pellet smokers and grills, although they can also be used for household heating. What makes wood pellets for cooking special, though, is that they come in flavors. And speaking of flavors, here is a quick wood pellet flavor guide for you:

Apple & Cherry Pellets: These pellets possess a smoky, mild, sweet flavor. They can enhance mild meat and are usually the go-to flavor for cooking pork or poultry. Despite being able to produce great smoke, these pellets are very mild.

Alder Pellets: This type of pellet is mild and neutral, but with some sweetness in it. If you're looking for something that provides a good amount of smoke but won't overpower delicate meat like chicken and fish, this is the flavor to go to.

Hickory Pellets: Hickory pellets produce a rich, Smokey, and bacon-like flavor. These are the pellets that are widely used for barbecue. Since this type of pellet is rich and Smokey, it can tend to be overwhelming. If that is the case, consider mixing it with apple or oak pellets.

Maple Pellets: If you are looking for something that is mild and comes with a hint of sweetness, maple pellets are the best option for you. They are great to use on turkey or pork.

Mesquite Pellets: A favorite option for Texas BBQ, mesquite pellets are characterized by a strong, spicy, and tangy flavor.

Oak Pellets: Oak pellets come in between apple and hickory. They are a bit stronger than the former and a bit milder than the latter and are an excellent choice when you're cooking fish or vegetables.

Pecan Pellets: Pecan is an all-time favorite. It's very similar to Hickory, but with a touch of vanilla, nutty flavor. The perfect pellets for beef and chicken, pecan pellets are very palatable and suits all occasions.

# COOKING TEMPERATURES, TIMES, AND DONENESS

With so many recipes to try with your pellet grill, it is easy to get overwhelmed right away. One important thing to keep in mind is that lower temperatures produce smoke, while higher temperatures do not. Follow this useful guide below to know the temperature and time it requires to get the perfectly flavored meat each time.

• Beef briskets are best cooked at 250 degrees using the smoke setting for at least 4 hours by itself and covered with foil for another 4 hours.

• Pork ribs should be cooked at 275 degrees on the smoke setting for 3 hours and covered with foil for another 2-3 hours.

• Steaks require 400-450 degrees for about 10 minutes on each side.

• Turkey can be cooked at 375 degrees for 20 minutes per pound of meat. For smoked turkey, the heat settings should be around 180-225 degrees for 10-12 hours or until the inside of the turkey reaches 165 degrees.

• Chicken breasts can be cooked at 400-450 degrees for 15 minutes on each side.

• A whole chicken cooks at 400-450 degrees for 1.5 hours or until the internal temperature reaches 165 degrees.

• Bacon and sausage can be cooked at 425 degrees for 5-8 minutes on each side.

• Hamburgers should be cooked at 350 degrees for at least 8 minutes for each side.

• You can smoke salmon for 1-1.5 hours and finish with a high setting for 2-3 minutes on each side.

• Shrimps cook at 400-450 degrees for 3-5 minutes on each side. If you prefer a smokier flavor, set the temperature at 225 degrees for about 30 minutes.

# ACCESSORIES NEEDED

You're off to a great start with your pellet grill, but there are a few other valuable tools that are well worthwhile to invest in. These tools appear throughout this cookbook – some are vital, and some simply elevate your repertoire.

Probe Meat Thermometer – If your grill doesn't have probe thermometers built-in, you 100% need to get one or two of them. They are crucial to almost any recipe, but especially for smoking recipes. Measuring your meat's internal temperature is the only way you can know when your food is safely cooked all the way through. It will also help you pull your food off of the cooker at your exact desired doneness.

BBQ Gloves – For your safety, it's best to have a pair of BBQ gloves just in case. Most of our recipes don't require BBQ gloves to safely handle your food, but some do. Plus, it never hurts to take extra caution when you're dealing with scorching hot temperatures.

Silicone Basting Brush – Many grill and smoker recipes utilize marinades that need to be brushed or basted onto your food. Basting brushes are quite affordable and a borderline necessity for any grilling toolbox.

Cast Iron Skillet – The cast iron skillet is one of the most versatile pans in any kitchen, and since pellet grills can bake, roast, and braise, we'll use them on the pellet grill too.

# HOW TO CLEAN YOUR GRILL

Just like every appliance, keeping your smoker clean is essential as well. If you neglect your appliance, it might slowly accumulate debris, oil, and drips, which might ultimately result in the appliance getting damaged.

The good idea is to keep a mixture of mild dish detergent and warm water handy as they are perfect when it comes to cleaning smokers. Alternatively, you may use non-abrasive cleaners as well should you choose.

A good tip is to clean your Smoker after every smoking session to avoid having a massive clean-up session down the road.

That being said, let me break down the necessary steps of cleaning your Smoker

Steps for cleaning the Smoker after every use:

• If you have used Wood Chips, make sure first to empty your smoker box and discard any ash. Carefully wipe the side of the box with a damp rag

• Next, remove the cooking racks, water pan, drip tray pan and wash them with warm soapy water, rinse and dry them

• As an added to apply a gentle coat of vegetable oil over the racks before your next smoking session for mess-free Smoking

• Remove the meat probe and clean it with a damp cloth as well

• Wipe the door seal with a damp cloth and get rid of any debris or residue

• Allow your Smoker to dry up before using again completely

Steps to keeping the outside of your Smoker clean

• Gently wipe the control panel on the top of your Smoker using a damp cloth with warm water, wipe it dry

• If your model has a window, then use approved cleaners suitable for ceramic glass cooktops to clean both the inside and outside of the window

Steps to cleaning the thermostats (If your device has it):

• Carefully wipe the surface of the two thermostats located on the reading inside of the wall of your Smoker using a soft, damp cloth

• Make sure to dip the cloth in warm soapy water before wiping, let them dry once done

Steps for cleaning the inside of your Smoker

• Make sure that your Smoker is wholly cooled off

• Take out the racks, water pan, drip tray, and smoker box

• Take a small brush/towel and brush any debris alongside the bottom and upper part of the Smoker

• Wipe any residue out of the chamber

• Use warm soapy water and carefully scrub the interior surfaces of the Smoker using a plastic bristle brush, wipe it dry once done

# Chapter 2

# BENEFITS OF THE WOOD PELLET SMOKER-GRILL

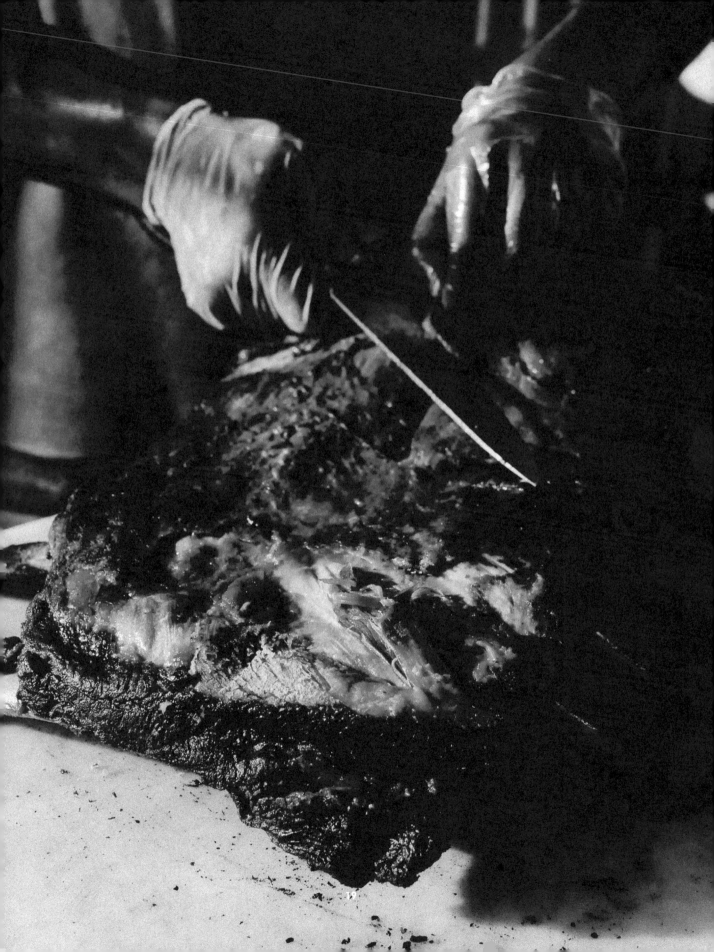

There are several advantages to using a wood pellet smoker-grill. Not only does it enhance the taste of your food, but it also offers several other benefits. Here are some of the biggest benefits of a wood pellet smoker-grill!

# SAVES TIME

It is a no-brainer that anything that saves time as well as effort, especially when it comes to cooking, deserves a warm welcome. One of the biggest advantages of using wood pellet grills is that they save you a lot of time. You can make your smoked dishes much faster and with much more ease and comfort. You can pre-heat them quickly, so you will save a lot of time.

# OFFERS VARIED COOKING OPTIONS

The best thing about wood pellet smoker-grills is that they give you several options for easy cooking. They are versatile and let you easily experiment with recipes and food. You can try various smoked recipes on the grill and enjoy healthy cooking. The versatility of pellet grills is probably one of their best qualities. This ensures that you can enjoy several lip-smacking recipes in a matter of minutes. In addition, you can use pellet grills for cooking all kinds of food, from braised short ribs to chicken wings.

# OFFERS VARIETY

Another significant advantage of using a wood pellet smoker-grill is that these smokers and grills come in a plethora of sizes and shapes. These grills are built and designed keeping the preferences, needs, and tastes of customers in mind. Therefore, people who are looking for convenient cooking tools can always find something for themselves in wood pellet smokers and grills. You can also choose from a wide range of flavors, such as maple, pecan, hickory, apple, and much more.

# COLD SMOKING

In addition to wood pellet fire grills and smokers, you can buy cold smokers from some companies. You can cook salmon and cheese dishes in these cold smokers.

# EASE OF USE

It is common to see many people get intimidated by the idea of using a pellet grill. However, those fears are unfounded. While a pellet grill is quite different from your standard charcoal grills or gas grills, they are surprisingly easy to use. These grills come with controls that users can set and then simply forget about. They come with several features that make the entire process of grilling a piece of cake.

These grills usually do not require any lighter fluid and they start with a single button. In addition, irrespective of the weather or the temperature outside, these grills can keep the temperature within a 10-degree range of your set temperature. This allows you to cook with zero effort like a pro. These grills are also designed to ensure that you do not overcook or over-smoke your food. Plus, they never flare-up. So, there is no need for you to worry about your beautiful eyebrows.

# VALUE

While pellet smokers are slightly more expensive than standard grills, this is for a good reason. As mentioned above, these pieces of equipment offer the perfect combination of a smoker and a grill. They come with solid construction and stainless-steel components. This is precisely why they also come with a nice four-year warranty.

This means that you will not buy these grills for sum-

mer only to dispose of them come winter. In addition, fuel efficiency is another one of their advantages. They come packed with double-wall insulation, which helps them sustain their temperatures better as well as use less fuel.

So, what are you waiting for? If you like to smoke or grill your food, it is not possible to go wrong with a good-quality pellet grill. They provide a wide range of advantages, such as their ease of use and the incredible flavor of your favorite smoked wood. Therefore, these grills are an amazing value for the money.

Keeping this in mind, let us dive right into some amazing tried-and-tested recipes using a wood pellet smoker-grill!

# KNOW YOUR MEAT

Choose the type of meat that tastes good with a smoky flavor. Following meat goes well for smoking.

Beef: ribs, brisket, and corned beef.

Pork: spareribs, roast, shoulder, and ham.

Poultry: whole chicken, a whole turkey, and big game hens.

Seafood: Salmon, scallops, trout, and lobster.

Getting Meat Ready

Prepare meat according to the recipe. Sometimes meat is cured, marinated, or simply seasoned with the rub. These preparation methods ensure smoked meat turns out flavorful, tender, and extremely juicy.

Brine is a solution to treating poultry, pork, or ham. It involves dissolving brine ingredients in water poured into a huge container and then adding meat to it. Then let soak for at least 8 hours and after that, rinse it well and pat dry before you begin smoking.

Marinate treat beef or briskets and add flavors to it. It's better to make deep cuts in meat to let marinate ingredients deep into it. Drain meat or smoke it straightaway.

Rubs are commonly used to treat beef, poultry, or ribs. They are a combination of salt and many spices, rubbed generously all over the meat. Then the meat is left to rest for at least 2 hours or more before smoking it.

Before smoking meat, make sure it is at room temperature. This ensures the meat is cooked evenly and reaches its internal temperature at the end of the smoking time.

# PLACING MEAT IN THE SMOKER

Do not place the meat directly overheat into the smoker because the main purpose of smoking is cooking meat at low temperatures. Set aside your fuel on one side of the smoker and place the meat on the other side and let cook.

Smoking time: The smoking time of meat depends on the internal temperature. For this, use a meat thermometer and insert it into the thickest part of the meat. The smoking time also varies with the size of the meat. Check recipes to determine the exact smoking time for the meat.

# BASTING MEAT

Some recipes call for brushing the meat with thin solutions, sauces, or marinade. This step not only makes meat better in taste, but also helps to maintain moisture in meat through the smoking process. Read the recipe to check out if basting is necessary.

Taking out meat: When the meat reaches its desired internal temperature, remove it from the smoker. Generally, poultry should be removed from the smoker when its internal temperature reaches 165 degrees F. For ground meats, ham, and pork, the internal temperature should be 160 degrees F. 145 degrees F is the internal temperature for chops, roast, and steaks.

# KNOW YOUR FISH

1. Choose Salmon, Swordfish, Tuna, Mahi-Mahi, Halibut, or Snapper

2. If you can't get fresh, look for "Frozen-At-Sea."

Your grilled fish recipe is only as good as your fish is fresh. If you're buying fresh, your local fishmonger or high-quality seafood grocer can give you fillets or steaks that should be firm to the touch and have a clean ocean smell. If your fish smells fishy in more ways than one, put it down and run away. Another alternative is to choose fish that is "Frozen at Sea." This can sometimes be better quality than fresh fish if you don't live near the water.

PREPPING YOUR FISH AND GRILL

3. Remove any pin bones, if your fishmonger hasn't already

These little bones can be pretty pesky while you're eating. To remove them, gently rub your fingers over the flesh. Pin bones will slightly poke out of the surface and are often located in the middle, meatiest part of the fish. You can easily remove them using needle-nose pliers.

4. Cook on clean and oiled grill grates

Clean your cooking grids to get great contact between your fish and the piping hot metal. In addition, the oil will season the cooking surface and prevent your masterpiece from sticking to the grids. Trust us, there's nothing worse than a perfectly grilled fish that ends up stuck to the cooking grids.

Add your high-smoke point oils, like canola, sunflower, or safflower - by using a spray, a paper towel, or rubbing the oil on an onion, and then rubbing the onion on the cooking surface.

5. Wait until your grill is nice and hot before you begin cooking

Most recipes will call for a medium to high temperature of 400°F to 450°F Letting the grill come up to temp prior to cooking will reduce the chance of sticking and shorten overall cook time

FISH COOKING TIPS

6. Grill using a foil packet

This is a foolproof method for easy cooking and amazing flavor. Foil packets also work particularly well for delicate fish that flake apart. Fold the foil so it creates a pouch to hold liquids and add in your fish, as well as, all your favorite flavors, like citrus, vinegar, soy sauce, olive oil, and other seasonings and rubs.

7. Wood Plank Grilling

Cedar planking is another surprisingly easy and fun to cook right on the grates. It also infuses hardwood flavor directly into the fish. Just be sure to soak the plank from 1 to 4 hours, prior to grilling. For an added touch, you can let both sides of the plank char and smolder for a minute prior to laying the fish on it to cook.

8. Add olive oil, or mayo if grilling fillets or steaks right on the grates

Mayo is an underrated, golden secret to deliciously grilled fish. It has a ton of oil and flavor. Mixed in with a few spices, it serves as the perfect pre and post grilling marinade. Just add a little of that or some go-to olive oil to both sides before searing.

9. Flip only once

Flipping only once, is another key to prevent your fish from falling apart. You know that it's time to flip when you see a nice brown crust on the outside.

A good rule of thumb is, 8 minutes of total grilling time, per 1 inch of thickness. So, look for signs to turn a 1-inch fillet or steak after 3-4 minutes.

FISH COOKING TIPS

10. Fish that's cooked properly should be opaque and flake easily

Fish can be tricky to track if it's covered in sauce or in a foil packet. However, when it comes to learning how to grill fish, it's important to know that overcooking fish is just as bad as overcooking anything else. It becomes dry or loses rich flavor and texture. Therefore, if you're not using an instant-read thermometer, it's totally ok to pull the fish off a little early to check that it's done to your liking

11. It's better to remove your fish a little early, rather than a little late

Fish can be tricky to track if it's covered in sauce or in a foil packet. However, when it comes to learning how to grill fish, it's important to know that overcooking fish is just as bad as overcooking anything else. It becomes dry or loses rich flavor and texture. Therefore, if you're not using an instant-read thermometer, it's totally ok to pull the fish off a little early to check that it's done to your liking

## Chapter 3.

# CHICKEN

# 170. SMOKED CHICKEN IN MAPLE FLAVOR

**Preparation Time:** 30 minutes

**Cooking Time:** 6 Hours

**Servings:** 1

## Ingredients:

**Boneless** chicken breast (5-lbs., 2.3-kgs)

**The** Spice

**Chipotle** powder – 1 tablespoon

**Salt** – 1 ½ teaspoons

**Garlic** powder – 2 teaspoons

**Onion** powder – 2 teaspoons

**Pepper** – 1 teaspoon

**The** Glaze

**Maple** syrup – ½ cup

**The** Fire

**Preheat** the smoker an hour prior to smoking.

**Use** charcoal and maple wood chips for smoking.

## Directions:

**1.** Preheat a smoker to 225°F (107°C) with charcoal and maple wood chips.

**2.** Place chipotle, salt, garlic powder, onion powder, and pepper in a bowl then mix to combine.

**3.** Rub the chicken with the spice mixture then place on the smoker's rack.

**4.** Smoke the chicken for 4 hours and brush with maple syrup once every hour.

**5.** When the internal temperature has reached 160°F (71°C), remove the smoked chicken breast from the smoker and transfer to a serving dish.

**6.** Serve and enjoy right away.

## Nutrition:

Carbohydrates: 27 g

Protein: 19 g

Sodium: 65 mg

Cholesterol: 49 mg

# 171. SOUTH-EAST-ASIAN CHICKEN DRUMSTICKS

**Preparation Time:** 15 minutes

**Cooking Time:** 2 hours

**Servings:** 6

## Ingredients:

**1** C. fresh orange juice

**¼** C. honey

**2** tbsp. sweet chili sauce

**2** tbsp. hoisin sauce

**2** tbsp. fresh ginger, grated finely

**2** tbsp. garlic, minced

**1** tsp. Sriracha

**½** tsp. sesame oil

**6** chicken drumsticks

## Directions:

**1.** Set the temperature of Grill to 225 degrees F and preheat with closed lid for 15 mins, using charcoal.

**2.** Mix all the ingredients except for chicken drumsticks and mix until well combined.

**3.** Set aside half of honey mixture in a small bowl.

**4.** In the bowl of remaining sauce, add drumsticks and mix well.

**5.** Arrange the chicken drumsticks onto the grill and cook for about 2 hours, basting with remaining sauce occasionally.

**6.** Serve hot.

## Nutrition:

Calories per serving: 385

Carbohydrates: 22.7g

Protein: 47.6g

Fat: 10.5g

Sugar: 18.6g

Sodium: 270mg

Fiber: 0.6g

## 172. GAME DAY CHICKEN DRUMSTICKS

|  |  |  |
|---|---|---|
| Preparation Time: 15 minutes | Cooking Time: 1 hour | Servings: 8 |

### Ingredients:

**For** Brine:

½ C. brown sugar

½ C. kosher salt

5 C. water

2 (12-oz.) bottles beer

8 chicken drumsticks

**For** Coating:

¼ C. olive oil

½ C. BBQ rub

1 tbsp. fresh parsley, minced

1 tbsp. fresh chives, minced

¾ C. BBQ sauce

¼ C. beer

### Directions:

**1.** For brine: in a bucket, dissolve brown sugar and kosher salt in water and beer.

**2.** Place the chicken drumsticks in brine and refrigerate, covered for about 3 hours.

**3.** Set the temperature of Grill to 275 degrees F and preheat with closed lid for 15 mins.

**4.** Remove chicken drumsticks from brine and rinse under cold running water.

**5.** With paper towels, pat dry chicken drumsticks.

**6.** Coat drumsticks with olive oil and rub with BBQ rub evenly.

**7.** Sprinkle the drumsticks with parsley and chives.

**8.** Arrange the chicken drumsticks onto the grill and cook for about 45 mins.

**9.** Meanwhile, in a bowl, mix together BBQ sauce and beer.

**10.** Remove from grill and coat the drumsticks with BBQ sauce evenly.

**11.** Cook for about 15 mins more.

**12.** Serve immediately.

### Nutrition:

Calories per serving: 448

Carbohydrates: 20.5g

Protein: 47.2g

Fat: 16.1g

Sugar: 14.9g

Sodium: 9700mg

Fiber: 0.2g

## 173. CAJUN CHICKEN BREASTS

|  | |  |
|---|---|---|
| Preparation Time: 10 minutes | Cooking Time: 6 hours | Servings: 6 |

### Ingredients:

2 lb. skinless, boneless chicken breasts

2 tbsp. Cajun seasoning

1 C. BBQ sauce

### Directions:

**1.** Set the temperature of Grill to 225 degrees F and preheat with closed lid for 15 mins.

**2.** Rub the chicken breasts with Cajun seasoning generously.

**3.** Put the chicken breasts onto the grill and cook for about 4-6 hours.

**4.** During last hour of cooking, coat the breasts with BBQ sauce twice.

**5.** Serve hot.

### Nutrition:

Calories per serving: 252

Carbohydrates: 15.1g

Protein: 33.8g; Fat: 5.5g

Sugar: 10.9g

Sodium: 570mg

Fiber: 0.3g

## 174. BBQ SAUCE SMOTHERED CHICKEN BREASTS

| Preparation Time: 15 minutes | Cooking Time: 30 minutes | Servings: 4 |
|---|---|---|

### Ingredients:

1 tsp. garlic, crushed

¼ C. olive oil

1 tbsp. Worcestershire sauce

1 tbsp. sweet mesquite seasoning

4 chicken breasts

2 tbsp. regular BBQ sauce

2 tbsp. spicy BBQ sauce

2 tbsp. honey bourbon BBQ sauce

### Directions:

**1.** Set the temperature of Grill to 450 degrees F and preheat with closed lid for 15 mins.

**2.** In a large bowl, mix together garlic, oil, Worcestershire sauce and mesquite seasoning.

**3.** Coat chicken breasts with seasoning mixture evenly.

**4.** Put the chicken breasts onto the grill and cook for about 20-30 mins.

**5.** Meanwhile, in a bowl, mix together all 3 BBQ sauces.

**6.** In the last 4-5 mins of cooking, coat breast with BBQ sauce mixture.

**7.** Serve hot.

### Nutrition:

Calories per serving: 421

Carbohydrates: 10.1g

Protein: 41,2g

Fat: 23.3g

Sugar: 6.9g

Sodium: 763mg

Fiber: 0.2g

## 175. CRISPY & JUICY CHICKEN

| Preparation Time: 15 minutes | Cooking Time: 5 hours | Servings: 6 |
|---|---|---|

### Ingredients:

¾ C. dark brown sugar

½ C. ground espresso beans

1 tbsp. ground cumin

1 tbsp. ground cinnamon

1 tbsp. garlic powder

1 tbsp. cayenne pepper

**Salt** and ground black pepper, to taste

1 (4-lb.) whole chicken, neck and giblets removed

### Directions:

**1.** Set the temperature of Grill to 200-225 degrees F and preheat with closed lid for 15 mins.

**2.** In a bowl, mix together brown sugar, ground espresso, spices, salt and black pepper.

**3.** Rub the chicken with spice mixture generously.

**4.** Put the chicken onto the grill and cook for about 3-5 hours.

**5.** Remove chicken from grill and place onto a cutting board for about 10 mins before carving.

**6.** Cut the chicken into desired-sized pieces and serve.

### Nutrition:

Calories per serving: 540

Carbohydrates: 20.7g

Protein: 88.3g

Fat: 9.6g

Sugar: 18.1g

Sodium: 226mg

Fiber: 1.2g

# 176. HOT AND SPICY SMOKED CHICKEN WINGS

| Preparation Time: 30 minutes | Cooking Time: 3 Hours | Servings: 1 |

**Ingredients:**

**Chicken** wings (6-lbs., 2.7-kgs)

**The** Rub

**Olive** oil – 3 tablespoons

**Chili** powder – 2 ½ tablespoons

**Smoked** paprika – 3 tablespoons

**Cumin** – ½ teaspoon

**Garlic** powder – 2 teaspoons

**Salt** – 1 ¾ teaspoons

**Pepper** – 1 tablespoon

**Cayenne** – 2 teaspoons

**The** Fire

**Preheat** the smoker an hour prior to smoking.

**Add** soaked hickory wood chips during the smoking time.

**Directions:**

**1.** Divide each chicken wing into two then place in a bowl. Set aside.

**2.** Combine olive oil with chili powder, smoked paprika, cumin, garlic powder, salt, pepper, and cayenne then mix well.

**3.** Rub the chicken wings with the spice mixture then let them sit for about an hour.

**4.** Meanwhile, preheat a smoker to 225°F (107°C) with charcoal and hickory wood chips. Prepare indirect heat.

**5.** When the smoker is ready, arrange the spiced chicken wings on the smoker's rack.

**6.** Smoke the chicken wings for 2 hours or until the internal temperature of the chicken wings has reached 160°F (71°C).

**7.** Take the smoked chicken wings from the smoker and transfer to a serving dish.

**8.** Serve and enjoy immediately.

**Nutrition:**

Carbohydrates: 17 g

Protein: 29 g

Sodium: 55 mg

Cholesterol: 48 mg

## 177. SWEET SMOKED CHICKEN IN BLACK TEA AROMA

|  |  |  |
|---|---|---|
| Preparation Time: 30 minutes | Cooking Time: 10 Hours | Servings: 1 |

### Ingredients:

**Chicken** breast (6-lbs., 2.7-kgs)

**The** Rub

**Salt** – ¼ cup

**Chili** powder – 2 tablespoons

**Chinese** five-spice – 2 tablespoons

**Brown** sugar – 1 ½ cups

**The** Smoke

**Preheat** the smoker an hour prior to smoking.

**Add** soaked hickory wood chips during the smoking time.

**Black** tea – 2 cups

### Directions:

**1.** Place salt, chili powder, Chinese five-spice, and brown sugar in a bowl then stir to combine.

**2.** Rub the chicken breast with the spice mixture then marinate overnight. Store in the refrigerator to keep it fresh.

**3.** In the morning, preheat a smoker to 225°F (107°C) with charcoal and hickory wood chips. Prepare indirect heat.

**4.** Pour black tea into a disposable aluminum pan then place in the smoker.

**5.** Remove the chicken from the refrigerator then thaw while waiting for the smoker.

**6.** Once the smoker has reached the desired temperature, place the chicken on the smoker's rack.

**7.** Smoke the chicken breast for 2 hours then check whether the internal temperature has reached 160°F (71°C).

**8.** Take the smoked chicken breast out from the smoker and transfer to a serving dish.

**9.** Serve and enjoy immediately.

### Nutrition:

Carbohydrates: 27 g
Protein: 19 g
Sodium: 65 mg
Cholesterol: 49 mg

## 178. SWEET SMOKED GINGERY LEMON CHICKEN

|  | | |
|---|---|---|
| Preparation Time: 30 minutes | Cooking Time: 6 Hours | Servings: 1 |

### Ingredients:

**Whole** chicken 2 (4-lbs., 1.8-kgs)

**Olive** oil – ¼ cup

**The** Rub

**Salt** – ¼ cup

**Pepper** – 2 tablespoons

**Garlic** powder – ¼ cup

**The** Filling

**Fresh** Ginger – 8, 1-inch each

**Cinnamon** sticks – 8

**Sliced** lemon – ½ cup

**Cloves** - 6

**The** Smoke

**Preheat** the smoker an hour prior to smoking.

**Add** soaked hickory wood chips during the smoking time.

### Directions:

**1.** Preheat a smoker to 225°F (107°C). Use soaked hickory wood chips to make indirect heat.

**2.** Rub the chicken with salt, pepper, and garlic powder then set aside.

**3.** Fill the chicken cavities with ginger, cinnamon sticks, cloves, and sliced lemon then brush olive oil all over the chicken.

**4.** When the smoker is ready, place the whole chicken on the smoker's rack.

**5.** Smoke the whole chicken for 4 hours then check whether the internal temperature has reached 160°F (71°C).

**6.** When the chicken is done, remove the smoked chicken from the smoker then let it warm for a few minutes.

**7.** Serve and enjoy right away or cut into slices.

### Nutrition:

Carbohydrates: 27 g
Protein: 19 g
Sodium: 65 mg
Cholesterol: 49 mg

# 179. HELLFIRE CHICKEN WINGS

|  |  |  |
|---|---|---|
| Preparation Time: 30 minutes | Cooking Time: 6 Hours | Servings: 1 |

## Ingredients:

**For** Hellfire chicken wings

**3** lbs. of chicken wings

**2** tablespoon of vegetable oil

**For** the rub

**1** teaspoon of onion powder

**1** tablespoon of paprika

**1** teaspoon of celery seed

**1** teaspoon of salt

**1** teaspoon of cayenne pepper

**1** teaspoon of freshly ground black pepper

**1** teaspoon of granulated garlic

**2** teaspoons of brown sugar

**For** the sauce

**2** -4 thinly sliced crosswise jalapeno poppers

**2** tablespoons of butter; unsalted

½ cup of hot sauce

½ cup of cilantro leaves

## Directions:

**1.** Take the chicken wings and cut off the tips and discard them

**2.** Now cut each of the wings into two separate pieces through the joint

**3.** Move this in a large mixing bowl and pour oil right over it

**4.** For the rub: Take a small-sized bowl and add sugar, black pepper, paprika, onion powder, salt, celery seed, cayenne, and granulated garlic in it

**5.** Now sprinkle this mixture over the chicken and toss it gently to coat the wings thoroughly

**6.** Put the smoker to preheat by putting the temperature to 350 degrees F

**7.** Grill the wings for approximately 40 minutes or till the time the skin turns golden brown and you feel that it has cooked through. Make sure to turn it once when you are halfway.

**8.** For the sauce: Take a small saucepan and melt the butter by keeping the flame on medium-low heat. Now add jalapenos to it and cook for 3 minutes, stir cilantro along with a hot sauce

**9.** Now, pour this freshly made sauce over the wings and toss it to coat well

**10.** Serve and enjoy

## Nutrition:

Carbohydrates: 27 g

Protein: 19 g

Sodium: 65 mg

Cholesterol: 49 mg

## 180. BUFFALO CHICKEN THIGHS

|  |  |  |
|---|---|---|
| Preparation Time: 30 minutes | Cooking Time: 6 Hours | Servings: 1 |

**Ingredients:**

4-6 skinless, boneless chicken thighs

**Pork** and poultry rub

4 tablespoons of butter

1 cup of sauce; buffalo wing

**Bleu** cheese crumbles

**Ranch** dressing

**Directions:**

**1.** Set the grill to preheat by keeping the temperature to 450 degrees F and keeping the lid closed

**2.** Now season the chicken thighs with the poultry rub and then place it on the grill grate

**3.** Cook it for 8 to 10 minutes while making sure to flip it once midway

**4.** Now take a small saucepan and cook the wing sauce along with butter by keeping the flame on medium heat. Make sure to stir in between to avoid lumps

**5.** Now take the cooked chicken and dip it into the wing sauce and the butter mix. Make sure to coat both the sides in an even manner

**6.** Take the chicken thighs that have been sauced to the grill and then cook for further 15 minutes. Do so until the internal temperature reads 175 degrees

**7.** Sprinkle bleu cheese and drizzle the ranch dressing

**8.** Serve and enjoy

**Nutrition:**

Carbohydrates: 29 g

Protein: 19 g

Sodium: 25 mg

Cholesterol: 19 mg

## 181. SWEET AND SOUR CHICKEN DRUMSTICKS

|  |  |
|---|---|
| Preparation Time: 30 minutes | Cooking Time: 2 Hours |

Servings: 1

**Ingredients:**

8 pieces of chicken drumsticks

2 tablespoon of rice wine vinegar

3 tablespoon brown sugar

1 cup of ketchup

¼ cup of soy sauce

**Minced** garlic

2 tablespoons of honey

1 tablespoon of sweet heat rub

**Minced** ginger

½ lemon; juice

1/2 juiced lime

**Directions:**

**1.** Take a mixing bowl and add soy sauce along with brown sugar, ketchup, lemon, rice wine vinegar, sweet heat rub, honey, ginger, and garlic.

**2.** Now keep half of the mixture for dipping sauce and therefore set it aside

**3.** Take the leftover half and pour it in a plastic bag that can be re-sealed

**4.** Now add drumsticks to it and then seal the bag again

**5.** Refrigerate it for 4 to 12 hours

**6.** Take out the chicken from the bag and discard the marinade

**7.** Fire the grill and set the temperature to 225 degrees F

**8.** Now smoke the chicken over indirect heat for 2 to 3 hours a make sure to turn it once or twice

**9.** Add more glaze if needed

**10.** Remove it from the grill and let it stand aside for 10 minutes

**11.** Add more sauce or keep it as a dipping sauce

**12.** Serve and enjoy

**Nutrition:**

Carbohydrates: 29 g

Protein: 19 g

Sodium: 25 mg

Cholesterol: 19 mg

# 182. SMOKED WHOLE CHICKEN WITH HONEY GLAZE

 Preparation
Time: 30 minutes

 Cooking Time:
3 Hours

 Servings:
1

## Ingredients:

1 4 pounds of chicken with the giblets thoroughly removed and patted dry

1 ½ lemon

1 tablespoon of honey

4 tablespoons of unsalted butter

4 tablespoon of chicken seasoning

## Directions:

1. Fire up your smoker and set the temperature to 225 degrees F

2. Take a small saucepan and melt the butter along with honey over a low flame

3. Now squeeze ½ lemon in this mixture and then move it from the heat source

4. Take the chicken and smoke by keeping the skin side down. Do so until the chicken turns light brown and the skin starts to release from the grate.

5. Turn the chicken over and apply the honey butter mixture to it

6. Continue to smoke it making sure to taste it every 45 minutes until the thickest core reaches a temperature of 160 degrees F

7. Now remove the chicken from the grill and let it rest for 5 minutes

8. Serve with the leftover sliced lemon and enjoy

## Nutrition:

Carbohydrates: 29 g
Protein: 19 g
Sodium: 25 mg
Cholesterol: 19 mg

# 183. BEER-BRAISED CHICKEN TACOS WITH JALAPENOS RELISH

|  |  | |
|---|---|---|
| Preparation Time: 30 minutes | Cooking Time: 3 Hours | Servings: 1 |

## Ingredients:

**For** the braised chicken

2 lbs. of chicken thighs; boneless, skinless

½ small-sized diced onion

1 de-seeded and chopped jalapeno

1 (12 oz) can of Modelo beer

1 tablespoon of olive oil

1 EA chipotle Chile in adobo

1 clove of minced garlic

4 tablespoon of adobo sauce

1 teaspoon of chili powder

1 teaspoon of garlic powder

1 teaspoon of salt

1 teaspoon of black pepper

**Juice** of 2 limes

**For** the tacos

**8-12** tortillas; small flour

**Hot** sauce

**Cilantro**

**Cotija** cheese

**For** the jalapeno relish

¼ cup of finely diced red onion

3 seeded and diced jalapenos

1 clove of minced garlic

1/3cup of water

1 tablespoon of sugar

2/3 cup of white wine vinegar

1 tablespoon of salt

**For** pickled cabbage

2 cups of red cabbage; shredded

½ cup of white wine vinegar

1 tablespoon of sugar

1 tablespoon of salt

## Directions:

**1.** For the jalapeño relish: take all the ingredients and mix then in a non-reactive dish and then keep it aside to be used.

**2.** For the pickled cabbage: take another non-reactive dish and mix all its respective ingredients and keep it aside

**3.** Now, transfer both the relish along with the pickled cabbage to your refrigerator and allow it to see for a couple of hours or even overnight if you so desire

**4.** Take the chicken thighs and season it with an adequate amount of salt and pepper

**5.** Take a Dutch oven and keep the flame over medium-high heat. Heat 1 tablespoon of olive oil in it. Now place the chicken thighs skin side down and brown

**6.** Remove them from the heat and then set it aside. Now, add 1 tablespoon of butter and keep the flame to medium-high

**7.** When the butter has melted, add jalapeno along with onion and sauté it for 3 to 5 minutes until they turn translucent. Add minced garlic to it and sauté it for 30 more seconds

**8.** Now add adobo sauce along with lime juice, chili powder, and chipotle chile. Add the chicken thighs in the oven and pour in the beer. Now set the grill to pre-heat by keeping the temperature to 350 degrees F

**9.** Place the oven on the grill and let it braise for 30 minutes. Remove the chicken from the braising liquid and slowly shred it

**10.** For the tacos: place the shredded part of chicken on the tortillas. Top it with jalapeno relish along with cotija, cabbage, and cilantro and pour the hot sauce. Serve and enjoy

## Nutrition:

Carbohydrates: 29 g

Protein: 19 g

Sodium: 25 mg

Cholesterol: 19 mg

# 184. SMOKED TERIYAKI CHICKEN WINGS WITH SESAME DRESSING

**Preparation Time:** 30 minutes

**Cooking Time:** 4 Hours

**Servings:** 1

## Ingredients:

Chicken wings

For the homemade Teriyaki Glaze:

2/3 cup mirin

2 tablespoons of minced ginger

3 tablespoons of cornstarch

2 tablespoon of rice vinegar

1 cup of soy sauce

1/3 cup of brown sugar

8 minced garlic cloves

2 teaspoon of sesame oil

3 tablespoons of water

For creamy sesame dressing:

1 green onion, chopped

1/2 cup of mayonnaise

1/4 cup rice wine vinegar

1 teaspoon of ground garlic

1 tablespoon of soy sauce

2 tablespoon of sesame oil

1/2 teaspoon of ground ginger

1 teaspoon siracha

2 tablespoon of maple syrup

Salt and pepper to taste

## Nutrition:

Carbohydrates: 39 g

Protein: 29 g

Sodium: 15 mg

Cholesterol: 19 mg

## Directions:

1. Use the light pellets for the sake of getting the smokey flavor

2. Set the grill to smoke mode by keeping the temperature to 225 degrees F

3. Now trim the wings and make them into drumettes and season with sea salt and black pepper

4. Smoke them for nearly 45 minutes

5. For the teriyaki glaze

6. Mince both garlic and ginger by using a teaspoon of sesame oil

7. Then mix all the ingredients except for cornstarch and water

8. Take a pan and boil cornstarch and water on low heat

9. Simmer for 15 minutes and then when done, mix it with an immersion blender

10. Now add cornstarch and water and stir it until it has mixed well

11. Add this mix to the teriyaki glaze and mix it well until it thickens. Set it aside

12. For the creamy dressing

13. Take a blender and blend all the ingredients thoroughly until you get a smooth mixture

14. Now set the grill for direct flame grilling and put the temperature to medium

15. Grill the wings for approx. 10 minutes

16. The internal temperature should reach 165 degrees F when you remove the wings from the grill

17. Toss them in the glaze when done

18. Sprinkle some sesame seeds along with green onion

19. Serve hot and spicy

# 185. SPICED LEMON CHICKEN

|  |  |  |
|---|---|---|
| Preparation Time: 30 minutes | Cooking Time: 5 Hours | Servings: 1 |

## Ingredients:

**1** whole chicken

**4** cloves of minced garlic

**Zest** of 2 fresh lemons

**1** tablespoon of olive oil

**1** tablespoon of smoked paprika

**1** ½ teaspoon of salt

½ teaspoon of black pepper

½ teaspoon of dried oregano

**1** tablespoon of ground cumin

## Directions:

**1.** Preheat the grill by pushing the temperature to 375 degrees F

**2.** Now take the chicken and spatchcock it by cutting it on both the sides right from the backbone to the tail via the neck

**3.** Lay it flat and push it down on the breastbone. This would break the ribs

**4.** Take all the leftover ingredients in a bowl except ½ teaspoon of salt and crush them to make a smooth rub

**5.** Spread this rub evenly over the chicken making sure that it seeps right under the skin

**6.** Now place the chicken on the grill grates and let it cook for an hour until the internal temperature reads 165 degrees F

**7.** Let it rest for 10 minutes

**8.** Serve and enjoy

## Nutrition:

Carbohydrates: 39 g

Protein: 29 g

Sodium: 15 mg

Cholesterol: 19 mg

# 186. SLOW ROASTED SHAWARMA

 Preparation
Time: 30 minutes

 Cooking Time:
4 Hours

 Servings:
1

## Ingredients:

**5 ½** lbs. of chicken thighs; boneless, skinless

**4 ½** lbs. of lamb fat

**Pita** bread

**5 ½** lbs. of top sirloin

**2** yellow onions; large

**4** tablespoons of rub

**Desired** toppings like pickles, tomatoes, fries, salad and more

## Directions:

**1.** Slice the meat and fat into ½" slices and place then in 3 separate bowls

**2.** Season each of the bowls with the rub and massage the rub into the meat to make sure it seeps well

**3.** Now place half of the onion at the base of each half skewer. This will make for a firm base

**4.** Add 2 layers from each of the bowls at a time

**5.** Make the track as symmetrical as you can

**6.** Now, put the other 2 half onions at the top of this

**7.** Wrap it in a plastic wrap and let it refrigerate overnight

**8.** Set the grill to preheat keeping the temperature to 275 degrees F

**9.** Lay the shawarma on the grill grate and let it cook for approx. 4 hours. Make sure to turn it at least once

**10.** Remove from the grill and shoot the temperature to 445 degrees F

**11.** Now place a cast iron griddle on the grill grate and pour it with olive oil

**12.** When the griddle has turned hot, place the whole shawarma on the cast iron and smoke it for 5 to 10 minutes per side

**13.** Remove from the grill and slice off the edges

**14.** Repeat the same with the leftover shawarma

**15.** Serve in pita bread and add the chosen toppings

**16.** Enjoy

## Nutrition:

Carbohydrates: 39 g

Protein: 29 g

Sodium: 15 mg

Cholesterol: 19 mg

# 187. DUCK POPPERS

 Preparation Time: 30 minu-tes

 Cooking Time:

4 Hours
Servings: 1

## Ingredients:

8 – 10 pieces of bacon, cut event into same-sized pieces measuring 4 inches each

3 duck breasts; boneless and with skin removed and sliced into strips measuring ½ inches

**Sriracha** sauce

6 de-seeded jalapenos, with the top cut off and sliced into strips

## Directions:

**1.** Wrap the bacon around one trip of pepper and one slice of duck

**2.** Secure it firmly with the help of a toothpick

**3.** Fire the grill on low flame and keep this wrap and grill it for half an hour until the bacon turns crisp

**4.** Rotate often to ensure even cooking

**5.** Serve with sriracha sauce

## Nutrition:

Carbohydrates: 39 g
Protein: 29 g
Sodium: 15 mg
Cholesterol: 19 mg

# 188. SMOKED DEVILED EGGS

 Preparation Time: 30 minutes

 Cooking Time: 4 Hours

Servings: 1

## Ingredients:

7 cooked and peeled eggs; hard-boiled

3 teaspoons of diced chives

2 teaspoons of crumbled bacon

3 tablespoons of mayonnaise

1 teaspoon of apple cider vinegar

1 teaspoon of brown mustard

**Dash** of hot sauce

**Salt** and pepper as per taste

**Paprika** for dusting

## Directions:

**1.** Set the grill to preheat with the temperature close to 180 degrees F

**2.** Now place the eggs that are cooked and peeled on the grill grate and then smoke them for 30 minutes

**3.** Remove from the grill and let it cool

**4.** Slice the eggs across their length and then scoop the yolk into a zip-top bag

**5.** Add chives along with the hot sauce, mayonnaise, vinegar, mustard, and salt and pepper to the zip-top bag.

**6.** Again, zip it closed and then knead all the ingredients in a way that they are mixed evenly and make a smooth paste

**7.** Now squeeze the mixture on to one corner of the bag and cut a very small part of the corner.

**8.** Drain off this mixture into hardboiled egg whites

**9.** Top these eggs with crumbled bacon and paprika

**10.** Chill it

**11.** Serve and enjoy

## Nutrition:

Carbohydrates: 19 g
Protein: 29 g
Sodium: 15 mg
Cholesterol: 59 mg

# 189. BAKED GARLIC PARMESAN WINGS

|  Preparation Time: 30 minutes |  Cooking Time: 3 Hours |  Servings: 1 |

## Ingredients:

**For** the chicken wings

**5lbs.** of chicken wings

½ cup of chicken rub

**For** the garnish

1 cup of shredded parmesan cheese

3 tablespoons of chopped parsley

**For** the sauce

**10** cloves of finely diced garlic

1 cup of butter

2 tablespoon of chicken rub

## Directions:

**1.** Set the grill on preheat by keeping the temperature to high

**2.** Take a large bowl and toss the wings in it along with the chicken rub

**3.** Now place the wings directly on the grill grate and cook it for 10 minutes

**4.** Flip it and cook for the ten minutes

**5.** Check the internal temperature and it needs to reach in the range of 165 to 180 degrees F

**6.** For the garlic sauce

**7.** Take a midsized saucepan and mix garlic, butter, and the leftover rub.

**8.** Cook it over medium heat on a stovetop

**9.** Cook for 10 minutes while stirring in between to avoid the making of lumps

**10.** Now when the wings have been cooked, remove them from the grill and place in a large bowl

**11.** Toss the wings with garlic sauce along with parsley and parmesan cheese

**12.** Serve and enjoy

## Nutrition:

Carbohydrates: 19 g

Protein: 29 g

Sodium: 15 mg

Cholesterol: 59 mg

# 190. GRILLED CHICKEN IN WOOD PELLETS

Preparation Time: 10 minutes

Cooking Time: 30 minutes

Servings: 8

## Ingredients:

**Whole** chicken - 4-5 lbs.

**Grilled** chicken mix

## Directions:

1. Preheat the wood pellet grill with the 'smoke' option for 5 minutes.

2. Preheat another 10 minutes and keep the temperature on high until it reaches 450 degrees.

3. Use baker's twine to tie the chicken's legs together.

4. Keep the breast side up when you place the chicken in the grill.

5. Grill for 70 minutes. Do not open the grill during this process.

6. Check the temperature of your grilled chicken. Make sure it is 165 degrees. If not, leave the chicken in for longer.

7. Carefully take the chicken out of the grill.

8. Set aside for 15 minutes.

9. Cut and serve.

## Nutrition:

Carbohydrates: 0 g
Protein: 107 g
Fat: 0 g
Sodium: 320 mg
Cholesterol: 346 mg

# 191. SMOKED CHICKEN LEG QUARTER IN A PELLET GRILL

|  |  |  |
|---|---|---|
| Preparation Time: 10 minutes | Cooking Time: 30 minutes | Servings: 8 |

**Ingredients:**

**Chicken** leg quarters - 4

**Dry** rub spice mix for chicken - 3 tablespoon

**Olive** oil - 1 tablespoon

**Salt**

**Directions:**

**1.** Wash and dry the chicken legs.

**2.** Add some olive oil. Sprinkle the dry rub spice mix all over the chicken.

**3.** Set aside for 20 minutes.

**4.** Preheat the grill on 'smoke' for 10-15 minutes.

**5.** Place the chicken on the grill with skin side up to smoke for 1 hour.

**6.** Increase the heat to 350 degrees and cook for another 30 to 60 minutes, depending on the size of the pieces and the number of chicken legs.

**7.** Poke into the thickest part of the thighs.

**8.** When done, serve one leg quarter with a side sauce of your choice.

**Nutrition:**

Carbohydrates: 1.5 g
Protein: 16 g
Fat: 21 g

# 192. GRILLED CHICKEN KEBABS

|  |  | |
|---|---|---|
| Preparation Time: 10 minutes | Cooking Time: 40 minutes | Servings: 8 |

**Ingredients:**

**For** Marinade

**Olive** oil - ½ cup

**Lemon** juice - 1 tablespoon

**White** vinegar - 2 tablespoon

**Salt** - 1 ½ tablespoon

**Minced** garlic - 1 tablespoon

**Fresh** thyme - 1 ½ tablespoon

**Fresh** Italian parsley - 2 tablespoon

**Fresh** chives - 2 tablespoon

**Ground** pepper - ½ tablespoon

**For** Kebabs

**Orange,** yellow, and red bell peppers

**Chicken** breasts - 1 ½, boneless and skinless

**Mushrooms** of your choice - 10-12 medium size

**Directions:**

**1.** Mix all the ingredients for the marinade.

**2.** Add the chicken and mushrooms to the marinade and put it in the refrigerator.

**3.** Preheat your wood pellet grill to 450 degrees.

**4.** Remove the marinated chicken from the refrigerator and place it on the grill.

**5.** Grill the kebabs on one side for 6 minutes. Flip to grill on the other side.

**6.** Serve with a side dish of your choice.

**Nutrition:**

Carbohydrates: 1 g
Fat: 2 g
Sodium: 582 mg

## 193. CHICKEN FAJITAS ON A WOOD PELLET GRILL

**Preparation Time:** 10 minutes

**Cooking Time:** 40 minutes

**Servings:** 1

### Ingredients:

**Chicken** breast - 2 lbs., thin sliced

**Red** bell pepper - 1 large

**Onion** - 1 large

**Orange** bell pepper - 1 large

**Seasoning** mix

**Oil** - 2 tablespoon

**Onion** powder - ½ tablespoon

**Granulated** garlic - ½ tablespoon

**Salt** - 1 tablespoon

### Directions:

**1.** Preheat the grill to 450 degrees.

**2.** Mix the seasonings and oil.

**3.** Add the chicken slices to the mix.

**4.** Line a large pan with a non-stick baking sheet.

**5.** Let the pan heat for 10 minutes.

**6.** Place the chicken, peppers, and other vegetables in the grill.

**7.** Grill for 10 minutes or until the chicken is cooked.

**8.** Remove it from the grill and serve with warm tortillas and vegetables.

### Nutrition:

Carbohydrates: 5 g

Protein: 29 g

Fat: 6 g

Sodium: 360 mg

Cholesterol: 77 mg

## 194. CHICKEN WINGS IN WOOD PELLETS

**Preparation Time:** 10 minutes

**Cooking Time:** 50 minutes

**Servings:** 1

### Ingredients:

**Chicken** wings - 6-8 lbs.

**Canola** oil – 1/3 cup

**Barbeque** seasoning mix - 1 tablespoon

### Directions:

**1.** Combine the seasonings and oil in one large bowl.

**2.** Put the chicken wings in the bowl and mix well.

**3.** Turn your wood pellet to the 'smoke' setting and leave it on for 4-5 minutes.

**4.** Set the heat to 350 degrees and leave it to preheat for 15 minutes with the lid closed.

**5.** Place the wings on the grill with enough space between the pieces.

**6.** Let it cook for 45 minutes or until the skin looks crispy.

**7.** Remove from the grill and serve with your choice of sides.

### Nutrition:

Protein: 33 g

Fat: 8 g

Sodium: 134 mg

Cholesterol: 141 mg

## 195. SMOKED CORNISH CHICKEN IN WOOD PELLETS

|  |  |  |
|---|---|---|
| Preparation Time: 10 minutes | Cooking Time: 50 minutes | Servings: 1 |

**Ingredients:**

**Cornish** hens - 6

**Canola** or avocado oil - 2-3 tablespoon

**Spice** mix - 6 tablespoon

**Directions:**

**1.** Preheat your wood pellet grill to 275 degrees.

**2.** Rub the whole hen with oil and the spice mix. Use both of these ingredients liberally.

**3.** Place the breast area of the hen on the grill and smoke for 30 minutes.

**4.** Flip the hen so the breast side is facing up. Increase the temperature to 400 degrees.

**5.** Cook until the temperature goes down to 165 degrees.

**6.** Pull it out and leave it for 10 minutes.

**7.** Serve warm with a side dish of your choice.

**Nutrition:**

Carbohydrates: 1 g
Protein: 57 g
Fat: 50 g
Sodium: 165 mg
Cholesterol: 337 mg

## 196. GRILLED FILET MIGNON

| Preparation Time: 10 minutes | Cooking Time: 20 minutes | Servings: 1 |
|---|---|---|

**Ingredients:**

**Salt**

**Pepper**

**Filet** mignon - 3

**Directions:**

**1.** Preheat your grill to 450 degrees.

**2.** Season the steak with a good amount of salt and pepper to enhance its flavor.

**3.** Place on the grill and flip after 5 minutes.

**4.** Grill both sides for 5 minutes each.

**5.** Take it out when it looks cooked and serve with your favorite side dish.

**Nutrition:**

Carbohydrates: 0 g
Protein: 23 g
Fat: 15 g
Sodium: 240 mg
Cholesterol: 82 mg

## 197. TANDOORI CHICKEN WINGS

| 🕐 | 🔥 | 👨‍🍳 |
|---|---|---|
| Preparation Time: 20 minutes | Cooking Time: 1 hour 20 minutes | Servings: 4-6 |

### Ingredients:

¼ Cup Yogurt

1 Whole Scallions, minced

1 Tablespoon minced cilantro leaves

2 Teaspoon ginger, minced

1 Teaspoon Masala

1 Teaspoon salt

1 Teaspoon ground black pepper

1 ½ pound chicken wings

¼ cup yogurt

2 tablespoon mayonnaise

2 tablespoon Cucumber

2 teaspoon lemon juice

½ teaspoon cumin

½ teaspoon salt

1/8 cayenne pepper

### Directions:

**1.** Combine yogurt, scallion, ginger, garam masala, salt, cilantro, and pepper ingredients in the jar of a blender and process until smooth.

**2.** Put chicken and massage the bag to cat all the wings

**3.** Refrigerate for 4 to 8 hours. Remove the excess marinade from the wings; discard the marinade

**4.** Set the temperature to 350F and preheat, lid closed, for 10 to 15 minutes. Brush and oil the grill grate

**5.** Arrange the wings on the grill. Cook for 45 to 50 minutes, or until the skin is brown and crisp and meat is no longer pink at the bone. Turn once or twice during cooking to prevent the wings from sticking to the grill.

**6.** Meanwhile combine all sauce ingredients; set aside and refrigerate until ready to serve.

**7.** When wings are cooked through, transfer to a plate or platter. Serve with yogurt sauce

### Nutrition:

Calories 241kcal

Carbohydrates 11g

Protein 12g

Fat 16g

Saturated Fat 3g

## 198. ASIAN BBQ CHICKEN

| 🕐 | 🔥 | 👨‍🍳 |
|---|---|---|
| Preparation Time: 12 to 24 h | Cooking Time: 1 hour | Servings: 4-6 |

### Ingredients:

1 whole chicken

To taste Asian BBQ Rub

1 whole ginger ale

### Directions:

**1.** Rinse chicken in cold water and pat dry with paper towels.

**2.** Cover the chicken all over with Asian BBQ rub; make sure to drop some in the inside too. Place in large bag or bowl and cover and refrigerate for 12 to 24 hours.

**3.** When ready to cook, set the Wood pellet grill to 372F and preheat lid closed for 15 minutes.

**4.** Open can of ginger ale and take a few big gulps. Set the can of soda on a stable surface. Take the chicken out of the fridge and place the bird over top of the soda can. The base of the can and the two legs of the chicken should form a sort of tripod to hold the chicken upright.

**5.** Stand the chicken in the center of your hot grate and cook the chicken till the skin is golden brown and the internal temperature is about 165F on an instant-read thermometer, approximately 40 minutes to 1 hour.

### Nutrition:

Calories 140kcal

Carbohydrates 18g

Protein 4g

Fat 4g

Sodium 806 mg

Potassium 682 mg

Fiber 5g

Sugar 8g

# 199. SMOKE ROASTED CHICKEN

| Preparation Time: 20 minutes | Cooking Time: 1 hour 20 minutes | Servings: 4-6 |

## Ingredients:

**8** tablespoon butter, room temperature

**1** clove garlic, minced

**1** scallion, minced

**2** tablespoon fresh herbs such as thyme, rosemary, sage or parsley

**As** needed Chicken rub

**Lemon** juice

**As** needed vegetable oil

## Directions:

**1.** In a small cooking bowl, mix the scallions, garlic, butter, minced fresh herbs, 1-1/2 teaspoon of the rub, and lemon juice. Mix with a spoon.

**2.** Remove any giblets from the cavity of the chicken. Wash the chicken inside and out with cold running water. Dry thoroughly with paper towels.

**3.** Sprinkle a generous amount of Chicken Rub inside the cavity of the chicken.

**4.** Gently loosen the skin around the chicken breast and slide in a few tablespoons of the herb butter under the skin and cover.

**5.** Cover the outside with the remaining herb butter.

**6.** Insert the chicken wings behind the back. Tie both legs together with a butcher's string.

**7.** Powder the outside of the chicken with more Chicken Rub then insert sprigs of fresh herbs inside the cavity of the chicken.

**8.** Set temperature to High and preheat, lid closed for 15 minutes.

**9.** Oil the grill with vegetable oil. Move the chicken on the grill grate, breast-side up then close the lid.

**10.** After chicken has cooked for 1 hour, lift the lid. If chicken is browning too quickly, cover the breast and legs with aluminum foil.

**11.** Close the lid then continue to roast the chicken until an instant-read meat thermometer inserted into the thickest part registers a temperature of 165F

**12.** Take off chicken from grill and let rest for 5 minutes. Serve, Enjoy!

## Nutrition:

Calories 222kcal

Carbohydrates 11g

Protein 29g

Fat 4g

Cholesterol 62mg

Sodium 616mg

Potassium 620mg

# 200. HOMEMADE TURKEY GRAVY

|  |  |  |
|---|---|---|
| Preparation Time: 20 minutes | Cooking Time: 3 hours 20 minutes | Servings: 8-12 |

## Ingredients:

**1** turkey, neck

**2** large Onion, eight

**4** celeries, stalks

**4** large carrots, fresh

**8** clove garlic, smashed

**8** thyme sprigs

**4** cup chicken broth

**1** teaspoon chicken broth

**1** teaspoon salt

**1** teaspoon cracked black pepper

**1** butter, sticks

**1** cup all-purpose flour

## Directions:

**1.** When ready to cook, set the temperature to 350F and preheat the wood pellet grill with the lid closed, for 15 minutes.

**2.** Place turkey neck, celery, carrot (roughly chopped), garlic, onion and thyme on a roasting pan. Add four cups of chicken stock then season with salt and pepper.

**3.** Move the prepped turkey on the rack into the roasting pan and place in the wood pellet grill.

**4.** Cook for about 3-4 hours until the breast reaches 160F. The turkey will continue to cook and it will reach a finished internal temperature of 165F.

**5.** Strain the drippings into a saucepan and simmer on low.

**6.** In a saucepan, mix butter (cut into 8 pieces) and flour with a whisk stirring until golden tan. This takes about 8 minutes, stirrings constantly.

**7.** Whisk the drippings into the roux then cook until it comes to a boil. Season with salt and pepper.

## Nutrition:

Calories 160kcal

Carbohydrate 27g

Protein 55g

Fat 23g

Saturated Fat 6.1g

# 201. GRILLED ASIAN CHICKEN BURGERS

| | | |
|---|---|---|
| Preparation Time: 5 minutes | Cooking Time: 50 minutes | Servings: 4-6 |

## Ingredients:

**Pound** chicken, ground

1 cup panko breadcrumbs

1 cup parmesan cheese

1 small jalapeno, diced

2 whole scallions, minced

2 garlic clove

¼ cup minced cilantro leaves

2 tablespoon mayonnaise

2 tablespoon chili sauce

1 tablespoon soy sauce

1 tablespoon ginger, minced

2 teaspoon lemon juice

2 teaspoon lemon zest

1 teaspoon salt

1 teaspoon ground black pepper

8 hamburger buns

1 tomato, sliced

**Arugula**, fresh

1 red onion sliced

## Nutrition:

Calories 329kcal

Carbohydrates 10g

Protein 21g

Fat 23g

## Directions:

**1.** Align a rimmed baking sheet with aluminum foil then spray with nonstick cooking spray.

**2.** In a large bowl, combine the chicken, jalapeno, scallion, garlic, cilantro, panko, Parmesan, chili sauce, soy sauce ginger, mayonnaise, lemon juice and zest, and salt and pepper.

**3.** Work the mixture with your fingers until the ingredients are well combined. If the mixture looks too wet to form patties and add additional more panko.

**4.** Wash your hands under cold running water, form the meat into 8 patties, each about an inch larger than the buns and about ¾" thick. Use your thumbs or a tablespoon, make a wide, shallow depression in the top of each

**5.** Put them on the prepared baking sheet. Spray the tops with nonstick cooking spray. If not cooking right away, cover with plastic wrap and refrigerate.

**6.** Set the pellet grill to 350F then preheat for 15 minutes, lid closed.

**7.** Order the burgers, depression-side down, on the grill grate. Remove and discard the foil on the baking sheet so you'll have an uncontaminated surface to transfer the slider when cooked.

**8.** Grill the burgers for about 25 to 30 minutes, turning once, or until they release easily from the grill grate when a clean metal spatula is slipped under them. The internal temperature when read on an instant-read meat thermometer should be 160F.

**9.** Spread mayonnaise and arrange a tomato slice, if desired, and a few arugula leaves on one-half of each bun. Top with a grilled burger and red onions, if using, then replace the top half of the bun. Serve immediately. Enjoy

## 202. CHICKEN BREAST WITH LEMON

 Preparation Time: 15min

 Cooking Time: 15min

Servings: 6

### Ingredients:

**6** Chicken breasts, skinless and boneless

**½** cup Oil

**1 - 2** Fresh thyme sprigs

**1** tsp. ground black pepper

**2** tsp. Salt

**2** tsp. of Honey

**1** Garlic clove, chopped

**1** Lemon the juice and zest

**For** service: Lemon wedges

### Directions:

**1.** In a bowl combine the thyme, black pepper, salt, honey, garlic, and lemon zest and juice. Stir until dissolved and combined. Add the oil and whisk to combine.

**2.** Clean the breasts and pat dry. Place them in a plastic bag. Pour the pre-made marinade and massage to distribute evenly. Place in the fridge, 4 hours.

**3.** Preheat the grill to 400F with the lid closed.

**4.** Drain the chicken and grill until the internal temperature reaches 165F, about 15 minutes.

**5.** Serve with lemon wedges and a side dish of your choice.

### Nutrition:

Calories: 230

Proteins: 38g

Carbohydrates: 1g Fat: 7g

---

## 203. PELLET SMOKED CHICKEN BURGERS

 Preparation Time: 20 minutes

 Cooking Time: 1 h +10 minutes

 Servings: 6

### Ingredients:

**2** lb. ground chicken breast

**2/3** cup of finely chopped onions

**1** Tbsps. of cilantro, finely chopped

**2** Tbsp. fresh parsley, finely chopped

**2** Tbsp. of olive oil

**1/2** tsp of ground cumin

**2** Tbsps. of lemon juice freshly squeezed

**3/4** tsp of salt and red pepper to taste

### Directions:

**1.** In a bowl add all ingredients; mix until combined well.

**2.** Form the mixture into 6 patties.

**3.** Start your pellet grill on SMOKE (oak or apple pellets) with the lid open until the fire is established. Set the heat to 350F and preheat, lid closed, for 10 to 15 minutes.

**4.** Smoke the chicken burgers for 45 - 50 minutes or until cooked through, turning every 15 minutes.

**5.** Your burgers are ready when internal temperature reaches 165 F

**6.** Serve hot.

### Nutrition:

Calories: 221

Carbohydrates: 2.12g

Fat: 8.5g

Fiber: 0.4g

Protein: 32.5g

## 204. PERFECT SMOKED CHICKEN PATTIES

| Preparation Time: 20 minutes | Cooking Time: 50 minutes | Servings: 6 |
|---|---|---|

### Ingredients:

**2** lb. ground chicken breast

**2/3** cup minced onion

**1** Tbsps. cilantro (chopped)

**2** Tbsp. fresh parsley, finely chopped

**2** Tbsp. olive oil

**1/8** tsp crushed red pepper flakes

**1/2** tsp ground cumin

**2** Tbsps. fresh lemon juice

**3/4** tsp kosher salt

**2** tsp paprika

**Hamburger** buns for serving

### Directions:

**1.** In a bowl combine all ingredients from the list.

**2.** Using your hands, mix well. Form mixture into 6 patties. Refrigerate until ready to grill (about 30 minutes).

**3.** Start your pellet grill on SMOKE with the lid open until the fire is established). Set the temperature to 350F and preheat for 10 to 15 minutes.

**4.** Arrange chicken patties on the grill rack and cook for 35 to 40 minutes turning once.

**5.** Serve hot with hamburger buns and your favorite condiments.

### Nutrition:

Calories: 258

Carbohydrates: 2.5g

Fat: 9.4g

Fiber: 0.6g

Protein: 39g

---

## 205. SMOKED CHICKEN BREASTS WITH DRIED HERBS

| Preparation Time: 15 minutes | Cooking Time: 40 minutes | Servings: 4 |
|---|---|---|

### Ingredients:

**4** chicken breasts boneless

**1/4** cup garlic-infused olive oil

**2** clove garlic minced

**1/4** tsp of dried sage

**1/4** tsp of dried lavender

**1/4** tsp of dried thyme

**1/4** tsp of dried mint

**1/2** Tbsps. dried crushed red pepper

**Kosher** salt to taste

### Directions:

**1.** Place the chicken breasts in a shallow plastic container.

**2.** In a bowl, combine all remaining ingredients, and pour the mixture over the chicken breast and refrigerate for one hour.

**3.** Remove the chicken breast from the sauce (reserve sauce) and pat dry on kitchen paper.

**4.** Start your pellet grill on SMOKE (hickory pellet) with the lid open until the fire is established). Set the temperature to 250F and preheat for 10 to 15 minutes.

**5.** Place chicken breasts on the smoker. Close pellet grill lid and cook for about 30 to 40 minutes or until chicken breasts reach 165F.

**6.** Serve hot with reserved marinade.

### Nutrition:

Calories: 391

Carbohydrates: 0.7g

Fat: 3.21g

Fiber: 0.12g

Protein: 20.25g

## 206. LEMON CHICKEN BREAST

 Preparation Time: 15 minutes

 Cooking Time: 30 minutes

 Servings: 4

**Ingredients:**

**6** chicken breasts, skinless and boneless

**½** cup oil

**1-3** fresh thyme sprigs

**1** teaspoon ground black pepper

**2** teaspoon salt

**2** teaspoons honey

**1** garlic clove, chopped

**1** lemon, juiced and zested

**Lemon** wedges

**Directions:**

**1.** Take a bowl and prepare the marinade by mixing thyme, pepper, salt, honey, garlic, lemon zest, and juice. Mix well until dissolved

**2.** Add oil and whisk

**3.** Clean breasts and pat them dry, place in a bag alongside marinade and let them sit in the fridge for 4 hours

**4.** Pre-heat your smoker to 400 degrees F

**5.** Drain chicken and smoke until the internal temperature reaches 165 degrees, for about 15 minutes

**6.** Serve and enjoy!

## 207. WHOLE ORANGE CHICKEN

 Preparation Time: 15 minutes + marinate time

 Cooking Time: 45 minutes

 Servings: 4

**Ingredients:**

**1** whole chicken, 3-4 pounds' backbone removed

**2** oranges

**¼** cup oil

**2** teaspoons Dijon mustard

**1** orange, zest

**2** tablespoons rosemary leaves, chopped

**2** teaspoons salt

**Directions:**

**1.** Clean and pat your chicken dry

**2.** Take a bowl and mix in orange juice, oil, orange zest, salt, rosemary leaves, Dijon mustard and mix well

**3.** Marinade chicken for 2 hours or overnight

**4.** Pre-heat your grill to 350 degrees F

**5.** Transfer your chicken to the smoker and smoke for 30 minutes' skin down. Flip and smoke until the internal temperature reaches 175 degrees F in the thigh and 165 degrees F in the breast

**6.** Rest for 10 minutes and carve

**7.** Enjoy!

**Nutrition:**

Calories: 230

Fats: 7g

Carbohydrates: 1g

Fiber: 2g

**Nutrition:**

Calories: 290

Fats: 15g

Carbohydrates: 20g

Fiber: 1g

# Chapter 4.

# TURKEY

## 228. APPLE WOOD-SMOKED WHOLE TURKEY

 Preparation Time: 10 minutes

 Cooking Time: 5 hours

Servings: 6

### Ingredients:

**1 (10- to 12-pound)** turkey, giblets removed

**Extra-virgin** olive oil, for rubbing

**¼** cup poultry seasoning

**8** tablespoons (1 stick) unsalted butter, melted

**½** cup apple juice

**2** teaspoons dried sage

**2** teaspoons dried thyme

### Directions:

**1.** Supply your smoker with wood pellets and follow the manufacturer's specific start-up procedure. Preheat, with the lid closed, to 250°F.

**2.** Rub the turkey with oil and season with the poultry seasoning inside and out, getting under the skin.

**3.** In a bowl, combine the melted butter, apple juice, sage, and thyme to use for basting.

**4.** Put the turkey in a roasting pan, place on the grill, close the lid, and grill for 5 to 6 hours, basting every hour, until the skin is brown and crispy, or until a meat thermometer inserted in the thickest part of the thigh reads 165°F.

**5.** Let the turkey meat rest for about 15 to 20 minutes before carving.

### Nutrition:

Calories: 180
Carbs: 3g
Fat: 2g
Protein: 39g

## 229. SAVORY-SWEET TURKEY LEGS

 Preparation Time: 10 minutes

 Cooking Time: 5 hours

Servings: 4

### Ingredients:

**1** gallon hot water

**1** cup curing salt (such as Morton Tender Quick)

**¼** cup packed light brown sugar

**1** teaspoon freshly ground black pepper

**1** teaspoon ground cloves

**1** bay leaf

**2** teaspoons liquid smoke

**4** turkey legs

**Mandarin** Glaze, for serving

### Directions:

**1.** In a huge container with a lid, stir together the water, curing salt, brown sugar, pepper, cloves, bay leaf, and liquid smoke until the salt and sugar are dissolved; let come to room temperature.

**2.** Submerge the turkey legs in the seasoned brine, cover, and refrigerate overnight.

**3.** When ready to smoke, remove the turkey legs from the brine and rinse them; discard the brine.

**4.** Supply your smoker with wood pellets and follow the manufacturer's specific start-up procedure. Preheat, with the lid closed, to 225°F.

**5.** Arrange the turkey legs on the grill, close the lid, and smoke for 4 to 5 hours, or until dark brown and a meat thermometer inserted in the thickest part of the meat reads 165°F.

**6.** Serve with Mandarin Glaze on the side or drizzled over the turkey legs.

### Nutrition:

Calories: 190
Carbs: 1g
Fat: 9g
Protein: 24g

# 230. HOISIN TURKEY WINGS

| Preparation Time: 15 minutes | Cooking Time: hour | Servings: 8 |
|---|---|---|

## Ingredients:

2 pounds turkey wings

½ cup hoisin sauce

1 tablespoon honey

2 teaspoons soy sauce

2 garlic cloves (minced)

1 teaspoons freshly grated ginger

2 teaspoons sesame oil

1 teaspoons pepper or to taste

1 teaspoons salt or to taste

¼ cup pineapple juice

1 tablespoon chopped green onions

1 tablespoon sesame seeds

1 lemon (cut into wedges)

## Directions:

**1.** In a huge container, combine the honey, garlic, ginger, soy, hoisin sauce, sesame oil, pepper and salt. Put all the mixture into a zip lock bag and add the wings. Refrigerate for 2 hours.

**2.** Remove turkey from the marinade and reserve the marinade. Let the turkey rest for a few minutes, until it is at room temperature.

**3.** Preheat your grill to 300°F with the lid closed for 15 minutes.

**4.** Arrange the wings into a grilling basket and place the basket on the grill.

**5.** Grill for 1 hour or until the internal temperature of the wings reaches 165°F.

**6.** Meanwhile, pour the reserved marinade into a saucepan over medium-high heat. Stir in the pineapple juice.

**7.** Wait to boil then reduce heat and simmer for until the sauce thickens.

**8.** Brush the wings with sauce and cook for 6 minutes more. Remove the wings from heat.

**9.** Serve and garnish it with green onions, sesame seeds and lemon wedges.

## Nutrition:

Calories: 115

Fat: 4.8g

Carbs: 11.9g

Protein 6.8g

# 231. TURKEY JERKY

|  |  |  |
|---|---|---|
| Preparation Time: 15 minutes | Cooking Time: 4 hours | Servings: 6 |

## Ingredients:
### Marinade:

**1** cup pineapple juice

**½** cup brown sugar

**2** tablespoons sriracha

**2** teaspoons onion powder

**2** tablespoons minced garlic

**2** tablespoons rice wine vinegar

**2** tablespoons hoisin

**1** tablespoon red pepper flakes

**1** tablespoon coarsely ground black pepper flakes

**2** cups coconut amino

**2** jalapenos (thinly sliced)

### Meat:

**3** pounds turkey boneless skinless breasts (sliced to ¼ inch thick)

## Directions:

**1.** Pour the marinade mixture ingredients in a container and mix until the ingredients are well combined.

**2.** Put the turkey slices in a gallon sized zip lock bag and pour the marinade into the bag. Massage the marinade into the turkey. Seal the bag and refrigerate for 8 hours.

**3.** Remove the turkey slices from the marinade.

**4.** Activate the pellet grill for smoking and leave lip opened for 5 minutes until fire starts.

**5.** Close the lid and preheat your pellet grill to 180°F, using hickory pellet.

**6.** Remove the turkey slices from the marinade and pat them dry with a paper towel.

**7.** Arrange the turkey slices on the grill in a single layer. Smoke the turkey for about 3 to 4 hours, turning often after the first 2 hours of smoking. The jerky should be dark and dry when it is done.

**8.** Remove the jerky from the grill and let it sit for about 1 hour to cool. Serve immediately or store in refrigerator.

## Nutrition:

Calories: 109

Carbs: 12g Fat:

1g Protein: 14g

# 232. SMOKED WHOLE TURKEY

|  |  | |
|---|---|---|
| Preparation Time: 20 Minutes | Cooking Time: 8 Hours | Servings: 6 |

## Ingredients:

**1** Whole Turkey of about 12 to 16 lb

**1** Cup of your Favorite Rub

**1** Cup of Sugar

**1** Tablespoon of minced garlic

**½** Cup of Worcestershire sauce

**2** Tablespoons of Canola Oil

## Directions:

**1.** Thaw the Turkey and remove the giblets

**2.** Pour in 3 gallons of water in a non-metal bucket of about 5 gallons

**3.** Add the BBQ rub and mix very well

**4.** Add the garlic, the sugar and the Worcestershire sauce; then submerge the turkey into the bucket.

**5.** Refrigerate the turkey in the bucket for an overnight.

**6.** Place the Grill on a High Smoke and smoke the Turkey for about 3 hours

**7.** Switch the grilling temp to about 350 degrees F; then push a metal meat thermometer into the thickest part of the turkey breast

**8.** Cook for about 4 hours; then take off the wood pellet grill and let rest for about 15 minutes

**9.** Slice the turkey, then serve and enjoy your dish!

## Nutrition:

Calories: 165

Fat: 14g

Carbs: 0.5g

Protein: 15.2g

# 233. SMOKED TURKEY BREAST

|  Preparation Time: 10 Minutes |  Cooking Time: 1 Hour 30 minutes | Servings: 6 |

## Ingredients:

**For** The Brine

**1** Cup of kosher salt

**1** Cup of maple syrup

**¼** Cup of brown sugar

**¼** Cup of whole black peppercorns

**4** Cups of cold bourbon

**1** and ½ gallons of cold water

**1** Turkey breast of about 7 pounds

**For** The Turkey

**3** Tablespoons of brown sugar

**1** and ½ tablespoons of smoked paprika

**1** ½ teaspoons of chipotle chili powder

**1** ½ teaspoons of garlic powder

**1** ½ teaspoons of salt

**1** and ½ teaspoons of black pepper

**1** Teaspoon of onion powder

**½** teaspoon of ground cumin

**6** Tablespoons of melted unsalted butter

## Directions:

**1.** Before beginning; make sure that the bourbon; the water and the chicken stock are all cold

**2.** Now to make the brine, combine altogether the salt, the syrup, the sugar, the peppercorns, the bourbon, and the water in a large bucket.

**3.** Remove any pieces that are left on the turkey, like the neck or the giblets

**4.** Refrigerate the turkey meat in the brine for about 8 to 12 hours in a reseal able bag

**5.** Remove the turkey breast from the brine and pat dry with clean paper towels; then place it over a baking sheet and refrigerate for about 1 hour

**6.** Preheat your pellet smoker to about 300°F; making sure to add the wood chips to the burner

**7.** In a bowl, mix the paprika with the sugar, the chili powder, the garlic powder, the salt, the pepper, the onion powder and the cumin, mixing very well to combine.

**8.** Carefully lift the skin of the turkey; then rub the melted butter over the meat

**9.** Rub the spice over the meat very well and over the skin

**10.** Smoke the turkey breast for about 1 ½ hours at a temperature of about 375°

## Nutrition:

Calories: 94

Fat: 2g

Carbs: 1g

Protein: 18g

# 234. WHOLE TURKEY

|  |  |  |
|---|---|---|
| Preparation Time: 10 Minutes | Cooking Time: 7 H + 30 Minutes | Servings: 10 |

## Ingredients:

**1** frozen whole turkey, giblets removed, thawed

**2** tablespoons orange zest

**2** tablespoons chopped fresh parsley

**1** teaspoon salt

**2** tablespoons chopped fresh rosemary

**1** teaspoon ground black pepper

**2** tablespoons chopped fresh sage

**1** cup butter, unsalted, softened, divided

**2** tablespoons chopped fresh thyme

**½** cup water

**14.5-ounce** chicken broth

## Directions:

**1.** Open hopper of the smoker, add dry pallets, make sure ash-can is in place, then open the ash damper, power on the smoker and close the ash damper.

**2.** Set the temperature of the smoker to 180 degrees F, let preheat for 30 minutes or until the green light on the dial blinks that indicate smoker has reached to set temperature.

**3.** Meanwhile, prepare the turkey and for this, tuck its wings under it by using kitchen twine.

**4.** Place ½ cup butter in a bowl, add thyme, parsley, and sage, orange zest, and rosemary, stir well until combined and then brush this mixture generously on the inside and outside of the turkey and season the external of turkey with salt and black pepper.

**5.** Place turkey on a roasting pan, breast side up, pour in broth and water, add the remaining butter in the pan, then place the pan on the smoker grill and shut with lid.

**6.** Smoke the turkey for 3 hours, then increase the temperature to 350 degrees F and continue smoking the turkey for 4 hours or until thoroughly cooked and the internal temperature of the turkey reaches to 165 degrees F, basting turkey with the dripping every 30 minutes, but not in the last hour.

**7.** When you are done, take off the roasting pan from the smoker and let the turkey rest for 20 minutes.

**8.** Carve turkey into pieces and serve.

## Nutrition:

Calories: 146

Fat: 8 g

Protein: 18 g

Carbs: 1 g

# 235. HERBED TURKEY BREAST

|  |  | |
|---|---|---|
| Preparation Time: 8 Hours And 10 Minutes | Cooking Time: 3 Hours | Servings: 1 2 |

## Ingredients:

**7** pounds turkey breast, bone-in, skin-on, fat trimmed

**3/4** cup salt

**1/3** cup brown sugar

**4** quarts water, cold

**For** Herbed Butter:

**1** tablespoon chopped parsley

**½** teaspoon ground black pepper

**8** tablespoons butter, unsalted, softened

**1** tablespoon chopped sage

**½** tablespoon minced garlic

**1** tablespoon chopped rosemary

**1** teaspoon lemon zest

**1** tablespoon chopped oregano

**1** tablespoon lemon juice

## Nutrition:

Calories: 97

Fat: 4 g

Protein: 13 g

Carbs: 1 g

## Directions:

**1.** Prepare the brine and for this, pour water in a large container, add salt and sugar and stir well until salt and sugar has completely dissolved.

**2.** Add turkey breast in the brine, cover with the lid and let soak in the refrigerator for a minimum of 8 hours.

**3.** Then remove turkey breast from the brine, rinse well and pat dry with paper towels.

**4.** Open hopper of the smoker, add dry pallets, make sure ash-can is in place, then open the ash damper, power on the smoker and close the ash damper.

**5.** Set the temperature of the smoker to 350 degrees F, let preheat for 30 minutes or until the green light on the dial blinks that indicate smoker has reached to set temperature.

**6.** Meanwhile, take a roasting pan, pour in 1 cup water, then place a wire rack in it and place turkey breast on it.

**7.** Prepare the herb butter and for this, place butter in a heatproof bowl, add remaining ingredients for the butter and stir until just mix.

**8.** Loosen the skin of the turkey from its breast by using your fingers, then insert 2 tablespoons of prepared herb butter on each side of the skin of the breastbone and spread it evenly, pushing out all the air pockets.

**9.** Place the remaining herb butter in the bowl into the microwave wave and heat for 1 minute or more at high heat setting or until melted.

**10.** Then brush melted herb butter on the outside of the turkey breast and place roasting pan containing turkey on the smoker grill.

**11.** Shut the smoker with lid and smoke for 2 hours and 30 minutes or until the turkey breast is nicely golden brown and the internal temperature of turkey reach to 165 degrees F, flipping the turkey and basting with melted herb butter after 1 hour and 30 minutes smoking.

**12.** When done, transfer the turkey breast to a cutting board, let it rest for 15 minutes, then carve it into pieces and serve.

# 236.  JALAPENO INJECTION TURKEY

|  | | |
|---|---|---|
| Preparation Time: 15 Minutes | Cooking Time: 4 H + 10 Minutes | Servings: 4 |

## Ingredients:

**15** pounds whole turkey, giblet removed

**½** of medium red onion, peeled and minced

**8** jalapeño peppers

**2** tablespoons minced garlic

**4** tablespoons garlic powder

**6** tablespoons Italian seasoning

**1** cup butter, softened, unsalted

**¼** cup olive oil

**1** cup chicken broth

## Directions:

**1.** Open hopper of the smoker, add dry pallets, make sure ash-can is in place, then open the ash damper, power on the smoker and close the ash damper.

**2.** Make the temperature of the smoker up to 200 degrees F, let preheat for 30 minutes or until the green light on the dial blinks that indicate smoker has reached to set temperature.

**3.** Meanwhile, place a large saucepan over medium-high heat, add oil and butter and when the butter melts, add onion, garlic, and peppers and cook for 3 to 5 minutes or until nicely golden brown.

**4.** Pour in broth, stir well, let the mixture boil for 5 minutes, then remove pan from the heat and strain the mixture to get just liquid.

**5.** Inject turkey generously with prepared liquid, then spray the outside of turkey with butter spray and season well with garlic and Italian seasoning.

**6.** Place turkey on the smoker grill, shut with lid, and smoke for 30 minutes, then increase the temperature to 325 degrees F and continue smoking the turkey for 3 hours or until the internal temperature of turkey reach to 165 degrees F.

**7.** When done, transfer turkey to a cutting board, let rest for 5 minutes, then carve into slices and serve.

## Nutrition:

Calories: 131

Fat: 7 g

Protein: 13 g

Carbs: 3 g

# 237. SMOKED TURKEY MAYO WITH GREEN APPLE

 Preparation
Time: 20 minutes

 Cooking Time: 4
hours 10 minutes

 Servings:
10

## Ingredients:

**Whole** turkey (4-lbs., 1.8-kg.)

**The** Rub

**Mayonnaise** – ½ cup

**Salt** – ¾ teaspoon

**Brown** sugar – ¼ cup

**Ground** mustard – 2 tablespoons

**Black** pepper – 1 teaspoon

**Onion** powder – 1 ½ tablespoons

**Ground** cumin – 1 ½ tablespoons

**Chili** powder – 2 tablespoons

**Cayenne** pepper – ½ tablespoon

**Old** Bay Seasoning – ½ teaspoon

**The** Filling

**Sliced** green apples – 3 cups

## Directions:

**1.** Place salt, brown sugar, brown mustard, black pepper, onion powder, ground cumin, chili powder, cayenne pepper, and old bay seasoning in a bowl then mix well. Set aside.

**2.** Next, fill the turkey cavity with sliced green apples then baste mayonnaise over the turkey skin.

**3.** Sprinkle the dry spice mixture over the turkey then wrap with aluminum foil.

**4.** Marinate the turkey for at least 4 hours or overnight and store in the fridge to keep it fresh.

**5.** On the next day, remove the turkey from the fridge and thaw at room temperature.

**6.** Meanwhile, plug the wood pellet smoker then fill the hopper with the wood pellet. Turn the switch on.

**7.** Set the wood pellet smoker for indirect heat then adjust the temperature to 275°F (135°C).

**8.** Unwrap the turkey and place in the wood pellet smoker.

**9.** Smoke the turkey for 4 hours or until the internal temperature has reached 170°F (77°C).

**10.** Remove the smoked turkey from the wood pellet smoker and serve.

## Nutrition:

Calories: 340

Carbs: 40g

Fat: 10g

Protein: 21g

# 238. BUTTERY SMOKED TURKEY BEER

| Preparation Time: 15 minutes | Cooking Time: 4 hours | Servings: 6 |

## Ingredients:

**Whole** turkey (4-lbs., 1.8-kg.)

**The** Brine

**Beer** – 2 cans

**Salt** – 1 tablespoon

**White** sugar – 2 tablespoons

**Soy** sauce – ¼ cup

**Cold** water – 1 quart

**The** Rub

**Unsalted** butter – 3 tablespoons

**Smoked** paprika – 1 teaspoon

**Garlic** powder – 1 ½ teaspoons

**Pepper** – 1 teaspoon

**Cayenne** pepper – ¼ teaspoon

## Directions:

**1.** Pour beer into a container then add salt, white sugar, and soy sauce then stir well.

**2.** Put the turkey into the brine mixture cold water over the turkey. Make sure that the turkey is completely soaked.

**3.** Soak the turkey in the brine for at least 6 hours or overnight and store in the fridge to keep it fresh.

**4.** On the next day, remove the turkey from the fridge and take it out of the brine mixture.

**5.** Wash and rinse the turkey then pat it dry.

**6.** Next, plug the wood pellet smoker then fill the hopper with the wood pellet. Turn the switch on.

**7.** Set the wood pellet smoker for indirect heat then adjust the temperature to 275°F (135°C).

**8.** Open the beer can then push it in the turkey cavity.

**9.** Place the seasoned turkey in the wood pellet smoker and make a tripod using the beer can and the two turkey-legs.

**10.** Smoke the turkey for 4 hours or until the internal temperature has reached 170°F (77°C).

**11.** Once it is done, remove the smoked turkey from the wood pellet smoker and transfer it to a serving dish.

## Nutrition:

Calories: 229

Carbs: 34g

Fat: 8g

Protein: 3g

# 239. BARBECUE CHILI SMOKED TURKEY BREAST

|  |  |  |
|---|---|---|
| Preparation Time: 15 minutes | Cooking Time: 4 hours 20 minutes | Servings: 8 |

## Ingredients:

**Turkey** breast (3-lb., 1.4-kg.)

**The** Rub

**Salt** – ¾ teaspoon

**Pepper** – ½ teaspoon

**The** Glaze

**Olive** oil – 1 tablespoon

**Ketchup** – ¾ cup

**White** vinegar – 3 tablespoons

**Brown** sugar – 3 tablespoons

**Smoked** paprika – 1 tablespoons

**Chili** powder – ¾ teaspoon

**Cayenne** powder – ¼ teaspoon

## Directions:

**1.** Score the turkey breast at several places then sprinkle salt and pepper over it.

**2.** Let the seasoned turkey breast rest for approximately 10 minutes.

**3.** In the meantime, plug the wood pellet smoker then fill the hopper with the wood pellet. Turn the switch on.

**4.** Set the wood pellet smoker for indirect heat then adjust the temperature to 275°F (135°C).

**5.** Place the seasoned turkey breast in the wood pellet smoker and smoke for 2 hours.

**6.** In the meantime, combine olive oil, ketchup, white vinegar, brown sugar, smoked paprika; chili powder, garlic powder, and cayenne pepper in a saucepan then stir until incorporated. Wait to simmer then remove from heat.

**7.** After 2 hours of smoking, baste the sauce over the turkey breast and continue smoking for another 2 hours.

**8.** Once the internal temperature of the smoked turkey breast has reached 170°F (77°C) remove from the wood pellet smoker and wrap with aluminum foil.

**9.** Let the smoked turkey breast rest for approximately 15 minutes to 30 minutes then unwrap it.

**10.** Cut the smoked turkey breast into thick slices then serve.

## Nutrition:

Calories: 290

Carbs: 2g

Fat: 3g

Protein: 63g

# 240. HOT SAUCE SMOKED TURKEY TABASCO

| Preparation Time: 20 minutes | Cooking Time: 4 hours 15 minutes | Servings: 8 |

## Ingredients:

**Whole** turkey (4-lbs., 1.8-kg.)

**The** Rub

**Brown** sugar – ¼ cup

**Smoked** paprika – 2 teaspoons

**Salt** – 1 teaspoon

**Onion** powder – 1 ½ teaspoons

**Oregano** – 2 teaspoons

**Garlic** powder – 2 teaspoons

**Dried** thyme – ½ teaspoon

**White** pepper – ½ teaspoon

**Cayenne** pepper – ½ teaspoon

**The** Glaze

**Ketchup** – ½ cup

**Hot** sauce – ½ cup

**Cider** vinegar – 1 tablespoon

**Tabasco** – 2 teaspoons

**Cajun** spices – ½ teaspoon

**Unsalted** butter – 3 tablespoons

## Directions:

**1.** Rub the turkey with 2 tablespoons of brown sugar, smoked paprika, salt, onion powder, garlic powder, dried thyme, white pepper, and cayenne pepper. Let the turkey rest for an hour.

**2.** Plug the wood pellet smoker then fill the hopper with the wood pellet. Turn the switch on.

**3.** Set the wood pellet smoker for indirect heat then adjust the temperature to 275°F (135°C).

**4.** Place the seasoned turkey in the wood pellet smoker and smoke for 4 hours.

**5.** In the meantime, place ketchup, hot sauce, cider vinegar, Tabasco, and Cajun spices in a saucepan then bring to a simmer.

**6.** Remove the sauce from heat and quickly add unsalted butter to the saucepan. Stir until melted.

**7.** After 4 hours of smoking, baste the Tabasco sauce over the turkey then continue smoking for 15 minutes.

**8.** Once the internal temperature of the smoked turkey has reached 170°F (77°C), remove from the wood pellet smoker and place it on a serving dish.

## Nutrition:

Calories: 160

Carbs: 2g

Fat: 14g

Protein: 7g

# 241. CURED TURKEY DRUMSTICK

|  |  | |
|---|---|---|
| Preparation Time: 20 minutes | Cooking Time: 2.5 / 3 hours | Servings: 3 |

## Ingredients:

3 fresh or thawed frozen turkey drumsticks

3 tablespoons extra virgin olive oil

**Brine** component

4 cups of filtered water

¼**Cup** kosher salt

¼ cup brown sugar

1 teaspoon garlic powder

**Poultry** seasoning 1 teaspoon

1/2 teaspoon red pepper flakes

1 teaspoon pink hardened salt

Directions:

**1.** Put the salt water ingredients in a 1 gallon sealable bag. Add the turkey drumstick to the salt water and refrigerate for 12 hours.

**2.** After 12 hours, remove the drumstick from the saline, rinse with

## Directions:

cold water, and pat dry with a paper towel.

**3.** Air dry the drumstick in the refrigerator without a cover for 2 hours.

**4.** Remove the drumsticks from the refrigerator and rub a tablespoon of extra virgin olive oil under and over each drumstick.

**5.** Set the wood pellet or grill for indirect cooking and preheat to 250 degrees Fahrenheit using hickory or maple pellets.

**6.** Place the drumstick on the grill and smoke at 250 ° F for 2 hours.

**7.** After 2 hours, increase grill temperature to 325 ° F.

**8.** Cook the turkey drumstick at 325 ° F until the internal temperature of the thickest part of each drumstick is 180 ° F with an instant reading digital thermometer.

**9.** Place a smoked turkey drumstick under a loose foil tent for 15 minutes before eating.

## Nutrition:

Calories: 278

Carbs: 0g

Fat: 13g

Protein: 37g

# 242. TAILGATE SMOKED YOUNG TURKEY

|  |  | |
|---|---|---|
| Preparation Time: 20 Minutes | Cooking Time: 4 / 4.30 Minutes | Servings: 6 |

## Ingredients:

1 fresh or thawed frozen young turkey

6 glasses of extra virgin olive oil with roasted garlic flavor

6 original Yang dry lab or poultry seasonings

## Directions:

**1.** Remove excess fat and skin from turkey breasts and cavities.

**2.** Slowly separate the skin of the turkey to its breast and a quarter of the leg, leaving the skin intact.

**3.** Apply olive oil to the chest, under the skin and on the skin.

**4.** Gently rub or season to the chest cavity, under the skin and on the skin.

**5.** Set up tailgate wood pellet smoker grill for indirect cooking and smoking. Preheat to 225 ° F using apple or cherry pellets.

**6.** Put the turkey meat on the grill with the chest up.

**7.** Suck the turkey for 4-4 hours at 225 ° F until the thickest part of the turkey's chest reaches an internal temperature of 170 ° F and the juice is clear.

**8.** Before engraving, place the turkey under a loose foil tent for 20 minutes

## Nutrition:

Calories: 240

Carbs: 27g

Fat: 9g

Protein: 15g

# 243. ROAST TURKEY ORANGE

| ⏱ | 🔥 | 👨‍🍳 |
|---|---|---|
| Preparation Time: 30 Minutes | Cooking Time: 2 hours 30 minutes | Servings: 6 |

## Ingredients:

**1** Frozen Long Island turkey

**3** tablespoons west

**1** large orange, cut into wedges

**Three** celery stems chopped into large chunks

**Half** a small red onion, a quarter

**Orange** sauce:

**2** orange cups

**2** tablespoons soy sauce

**2** tablespoons orange marmalade

**2** tablespoons honey

**3** teaspoons grated raw

## Nutrition:

Calories: 216

Carbs: 2g

Fat: 11g

Protein: 34g

## Directions:

**1.** Remove the nibble from the turkey's cavity and neck and retain or discard for another use. Wash the duck and pat some dry paper towel.

**2.** Remove excess fat from tail, neck and cavity. Use a sharp scalpel knife tip to pierce the turkey's skin entirely, so that it does not penetrate the duck's meat, to help dissolve the fat layer beneath the skin.

**3.** Add the seasoning inside the cavity with one cup of rub or seasoning.

**4.** Season the outside of the turkey with the remaining friction or seasoning.

**5.** Fill the cavity with orange wedges, celery and onion. Duck legs are tied with butcher twine to make filling easier. Place the turkey's breast up on a small rack of shallow roast bread.

**6.** To make the sauce, mix the ingredients in the saucepan over low heat and cook until the sauce is thick and syrupy. Set aside and let cool.

**7.** Set the wood pellet smoker grill for indirect cooking and use the pellets to preheat to 350 ° F.

**8.** Roast the turkey at 350 ° F for 2 hours.

**9.** After 2 hours, brush the turkey freely with orange sauce.

**10.** Roast the orange glass turkey for another 30 minutes, making sure that the inside temperature of the thickest part of the leg reaches 165 ° F.

**11.** Place turkey under loose foil tent for 20 minutes before serving.

**12.** Discard the orange wedge, celery and onion. Serve with a quarter of turkey with poultry scissors.

# 244. THANKSGIVING DINNER TURKEY

**Preparation Time:** 15 minutes

**Cooking Time:** 4 hours

**Servings:** 16

## Ingredients:

½ lb. butter, softened

**2** tbsp. fresh thyme, chopped

**2** tbsp. fresh rosemary, chopped

**6** garlic cloves, crushed

**1** (20-lb.) whole turkey, neck and giblets removed

**Salt** and ground black pepper

## Directions:

**1.** Set the temperature of Grill to 300 degrees F and preheat with closed lid for 15 mins, using charcoal.

**2.** In a bowl, place butter, fresh herbs, garlic, salt and black pepper and mix well.

**3.** Separate the turkey skin from breast to create a pocket.

**4.** Stuff the breast pocket with ¼-inch thick layer of butter mixture.

**5.** Season turkey with salt and black pepper.

**6.** Arrange the turkey onto the grill and cook for 3-4 hours.

**7.** Remove the turkey from grill and place onto a cutting board for about 15-20 mins before carving.

**8.** Cut the turkey into desired-sized pieces and serve.

## Nutrition:

Calories per serving: 965

Carbohydrates: 0.6;

Protein: 106.5g

Fat: 52g

Sugar: 0g

Sodium: 1916mg

Fiber: 0.2g

# 245. HERB ROASTED TURKEY

|  Preparation Time: 15 Minutes |  Cooking Time: 3 Hours 30 Minutes |  Servings: 12 |
|---|---|---|

## Ingredients:

**14** pounds turkey, cleaned

**2** tablespoons chopped mixed herbs

**Pork** and poultry rub as needed

**¼** teaspoon ground black pepper

**3** tablespoons butter, unsalted, melted

**8** tablespoons butter, unsalted, softened

**2** cups chicken broth

## Directions:

**1.** Clean the turkey by removing the giblets, wash it inside out, pat dry with paper towels, then place it on a roasting pan and tuck the turkey wings by tiring with butcher's string.

**2.** Switch on the grill, fill the grill hopper with hickory flavored wood pellets, power the grill on by using the control panel, select 'smoke' on the temperature dial, or set the temperature to 325 degrees F and let it preheat for a minimum of 15 minutes.

**3.** Meanwhile, prepared herb butter and for this, take a small bowl, place the softened butter in it, add black pepper and mixed herbs and beat until fluffy.

**4.** Place some of the prepared herb butter underneath the skin of turkey by using a handle of a wooden spoon, and massage the skin to distribute butter evenly.

**5.** Then rub the exterior of the turkey with melted butter, season with pork and poultry rub, and pour the broth in the roasting pan.

**6.** When the grill has preheated, open the lid, place roasting pan containing turkey on the grill grate, shut the grill and smoke for 3 hours and 30 minutes until the internal temperature reaches 165 degrees F and the top has turned golden brown.

**7.** When done, transfer turkey to a cutting board, let it rest for 30 minutes, then carve it into slices and serve.

## Nutrition:

Calories: 154.6 Fat: 3.1 g
Carbs: 8.4 g Protein: 28.8 g

# 246. TURKEY LEGS

| Preparation Time: 10 Minutes | Cooking Time: 5 Hours | Servings: 4 |
|---|---|---|

## Ingredients:

**4** turkey legs

**For** the Brine:

**½** cup curing salt

**1** tablespoon whole black peppercorns

**1** cup BBQ rub

**½** cup brown sugar

**2** bay leaves

**2** teaspoons liquid smoke

**16** cups of warm water

**4** cups ice

**8** cups of cold water

## Directions:

**1.** Prepare the brine and for this, take a large stockpot, place it over high heat, pour warm water in it, add peppercorn, bay leaves, and liquid smoke, stir in salt, sugar, and BBQ rub and bring it to a boil.

**2.** Remove pot from heat, bring it to room temperature, then pour in cold water, add ice cubes and let the brine chill in the refrigerator.

**3.** Then add turkey legs in it, submerge them completely, and let soak for 24 hours in the refrigerator.

**4.** After 24 hours, remove turkey legs from the brine, rinse well and pat dry with paper towels.

**5.** When ready to cook, switch on the grill, fill the grill hopper with hickory flavored wood pellets, power the grill on by using the control panel, select 'smoke' on the temperature dial, or set the temperature to 250 degrees F and let it preheat for a minimum of 15 minutes.

**6.** When the grill has preheated, open the lid, place turkey legs on the grill grate, shut the grill, and smoke for 5 hours until nicely browned and the internal temperature reaches 165 degrees F. Serve immediately.

## Nutrition:

Calories: 416
Fat: 13.3 g
Carbs: 0 g
Protein: 69.8 g

# 247. TURKEY BREAST

| Preparation Time: 12 Hours | Cooking Time: 8 Hours | Servings: 6 |
|---|---|---|

## Ingredients:

**For** the Brine:

2 pounds turkey breast, deboned

2 tablespoons ground black pepper

¼ cup salt

1 cup brown sugar

4 cups cold water

**For** the BBQ Rub:

2 tablespoons dried onions

2 tablespoons garlic powder

¼ cup paprika

2 tablespoons ground black pepper

1 tablespoon salt

2 tablespoons brown sugar

2 tablespoons red chili powder

1 tablespoon cayenne pepper

2 tablespoons sugar

2 tablespoons ground cumin

## Directions:

**1.** Prepare the brine and for this, take a large bowl, add salt, black pepper, and sugar in it, pour in water, and stir until sugar has dissolved.

**2.** Place turkey breast in it, submerge it completely and let it soak for a minimum of 12 hours in the refrigerator.

**3.** Meanwhile, prepare the BBQ rub and for this, take a small bowl, place all of its ingredients in it and then stir until combined, set aside until required.

**4.** Then remove turkey breast from the brine and season well with the prepared BBQ rub.

**5.** When ready to cook, switch on the grill, fill the grill hopper with apple-flavored wood pellets, power the grill on by using the control panel, select 'smoke' on the temperature dial, or set the temperature to 180 degrees F and let it preheat for a minimum of 15 minutes.

**6.** When the grill has preheated, open the lid, place turkey breast on the grill grate, shut the grill, change the smoking temperature to 225 degrees F, and smoke for 8 hours until the internal temperature reaches 160 degrees F.

**7.** When done, transfer turkey to a cutting board, let it rest for 10 minutes, then cut it into slices and serve.

## Nutrition:

Calories: 250

Fat: 5 g

Carbs: 31 g

Protein: 18 g

# 248. MARINATED SMOKED TURKEY BREAST

|  |  |  |
|---|---|---|
| Preparation Time: 15 minutes | Cooking Time: 4 hours | Servings: 6 |

## Ingredients:

**1** (5 pounds) boneless chicken breast

**4** cups water

**2** tablespoons kosher salt

**1** teaspoon Italian seasoning

**2** tablespoons honey

**1** tablespoon cider vinegar

### Rub:

**½** teaspoon onion powder

**1** teaspoon paprika

**1** teaspoon salt

**1** teaspoon ground black pepper

**1** tablespoons brown sugar

**½** teaspoon garlic powder

**1** teaspoon oregano

## Directions:

**1.** In a huge container, combine the water, honey, cider vinegar, Italian seasoning and salt.

**2.** Add the chicken breast and toss to combine. Cover the bowl and place it in the refrigerator and chill for 4 hours.

**3.** Rinse the chicken breast with water and pat dry with paper towels.

**4.** In another mixing bowl, combine the brown sugar, salt, paprika, onion powder, pepper, oregano and garlic.

**5.** Generously season the chicken breasts with the rub mix.

**6.** Preheat the grill to 225°F with lid closed for 15 minutes. Use cherry wood pellets.

**7.** Arrange the turkey breast into a grill rack. Place the grill rack on the grill.

**8.** Smoke for about 3 to 4 hours or until the internal temperature of the turkey breast reaches 165°F.

**9.** Remove the chicken breast from heat and let them rest for a few minutes. Serve.

## Nutrition:

Calories 903

Fat: 34g

Carbs: 9.9g

Protein 131.5g

# 249. SMOKED TURKEY PATTIES

|  |  | |
|---|---|---|
| Preparation Time: 20 minutes | Cooking Time: 40 minutes | Servings: 6 |

## Ingredients:

**2** lbs. turkey minced meat

**1/2** cup of parsley finely chopped

**2/3** cup of onion finely chopped

**1** red bell pepper finely chopped

**1** large egg at room temperature

**Salt** and pepper to taste

**1/2** tsp dry oregano

**1/2** tsp dry thyme

## Directions:

**1.** In a bowl, combine well all ingredients.

**2.** Make from the mixture patties.

**3.** Start pellet grill on (recommended apple or oak pellet) lid open, until the fire is established (4-5 minutes). Increase the temperature to 350F and allow to pre-heat, lid closed, for 10 - 15 minutes.

**4.** Place patties on the grill racks and cook with lid covered for 30 to 40 minutes.

**5.** Your turkey patties are ready when you reach a temperature of 130F

**6.** Serve hot.

## Nutrition:

Calories: 251

Carbohydrates: 3.4g

Fat: 12.5

Fiber: 0.9g

Protein: 31.2g

# 250. MAPLE BOURBON TURKEY

|  |  |  |
|---|---|---|
| Preparation Time: 15 minutes | Cooking Time: 3 hours | Servings: 8 |

## Ingredients:

1 (12 pounds) turkey

8 cup chicken broth

1 stick butter (softened)

1 teaspoon thyme

2 garlic clove (minced)

1 teaspoon dried basil

1 teaspoon pepper

1 teaspoon salt

1 tablespoon minced rosemary

1 teaspoon paprika

1 lemon (wedged)

1 onion

1 orange (wedged)

1 apple (wedged)

**Maple** Bourbon Glaze:

¾ cup bourbon

1/2 cup maple syrup

1 stick butter (melted)

1 tablespoon lime

## Directions:

**1.** Wash the turkey meat inside and out under cold running water.

**2.** Insert the onion, lemon, orange and apple into the turkey cavity.

**3.** In a mixing bowl, combine the butter, paprika, thyme, garlic, basil, pepper, salt, basil and rosemary.

**4.** Brush the turkey generously with the herb butter mixture.

**5.** Set a rack into a roasting pan and place the turkey on the rack. Put a 5 cups of chicken broth into the bottom of the roasting pan.

**6.** Preheat the grill to 350°F with lid closed for 15 minutes, using maple wood pellets.

**7.** Place the roasting pan in the grill and cook for 1 hour.

**8.** Meanwhile, combine all the maple bourbon glaze ingredients in a mixing bowl. Mix until well combined.

**9.** Baste the turkey with glaze mixture. Continue cooking, basting turkey every 30 minutes and adding more broth as needed for 2 hours, or until the internal temperature of the turkey reaches 165°F.

**10.** Take off the turkey from the grill and let it rest for a few minutes. Cut into slices and serve.

## Nutrition:

Calories 1536

Fat 58.6g

Carbs: 24g

Protein 20.1g

# 251. APPLE SMOKED TURKEY

|  |  |  |
|---|---|---|
| Preparation Time: 30 Minutes | Cooking Time: 3 Hours | Servings: 5 |

## Ingredients:

**4** Cups Apple wood chips

**1** Fresh or frozen turkey of about 12 pounds

**3** Tablespoons of extra-virgin olive oil

**1** tablespoon of chopped fresh sage

**2** and ½ teaspoons of kosher salt

**2** Teaspoons of freshly ground black pepper

**1** and ½ teaspoons of paprika

**1** Teaspoon of chopped fresh thyme

**1** Teaspoon of chopped fresh oregano

**1** Teaspoon of garlic powder

**1** Cup of water

½ Cup of chopped onion

½ Cup of chopped carrot

½ Cup of chopped celery

## Nutrition:

Calories: 530,

Fat: 22g,

Carbohydrates: 14g,

Protein: 41g,

Dietary Fiber 2g

## Directions:

**1.** Soak the wood chips into the water for about 1 hour; then drain very well.

**2.** Remove the neck and the giblets from the turkey; then reserve and discard the liver. Pat the turkey dry; then trim any excess of fat and start at the neck's cavity

**3.** Loosen the skin from the breast and the drumstick by inserting your fingers and gently push it between the meat and skin and lift the wingtips, then over back and tuck under the turkey

**4.** Combine the oil and the next 7 ingredients in a medium bowl and rub the oil under the skin; then rub it over the breasts and the drumsticks

**5.** Tie the legs with the kitchen string.

**6.** Pour 1 cup of water, the onion, the carrot, and the celery into the bottom of an aluminum foil roasting pan

**7.** Place the roasting rack into a pan; then arrange the turkey with the breast side up over a roasting rack; then let stand at the room temperature for about 1 hour

**8.** Remove the grill rack; then preheat the charcoal smoker grill to medium-high heat.

**9.** After preheating the smoker to a temperature of about 225°F

**10.** Place 2 cups of wood chips on the heating element on the right side.

**11.** Replace the grill rack; then place the roasting pan with the turkey over the grill rack over the left burner.

**12.** Cover and smoke for about 3 hours and turn the chicken halfway through the cooking time; then add the remaining 2 cups of wood chips halfway through the cooking time.

**13.** Place the turkey over a cutting board; then let stand for about 30 minutes

**14.** Discard the turkey skin; then serve and enjoy your dish!

# 252. WILD TURKEY EGG ROLLS

|  | 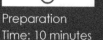 |  |
|---|---|---|
| Preparation Time: 10 minutes | Cooking Time: 55 minutes | Servings: 1 |

## Ingredients:

**Corn** - ½ cup

**Leftover** wild turkey meat - 2 cups

**Black** beans - ½ cup

**Taco** seasoning - 3 tablespoon

**Water** ½ cup

**Rotel** chilies and tomatoes - 1 can

**Egg** roll wrappers- 12

**Cloves** of minced garlic- 4

**1** chopped Poblano pepper or 2 jalapeno peppers

**Chopped** white onion - ½ cup

## Directions:

**1.** Add some olive oil to a fairly large skillet. Heat it over medium heat on a stove.

**2.** Add peppers and onions. Sauté the mixture for 2-3 minutes until it turns soft.

**3.** Add some garlic and sauté for another 30 seconds. Add the Rotel chilies and beans to the mixture. Keeping mixing the content gently. Reduce the heat and then simmer.

**4.** After about 4-5 minutes, pour in the taco seasoning and 1/3 cup of water over the meat. Mix everything and coat the meat well. If you feel that it is a bit dry, you can add 2 tablespoons of water. Keep cooking until everything is heated all the way through.

**5.** Remove the content from the heat and box it to store in a refrigerator. Before you stuff the mixture into the egg wrappers, it should be completely cool to avoid breaking the rolls.

**6.** Place a spoonful of the cooked mixture in each wrapper and then wrap it securely and tightly. Do the same with all the wrappers.

**7.** Preheat the pellet grill and brush it with some oil. Cook the egg rolls for 15 minutes on both sides, until the exterior is nice and crispy.

**8.** Remove them from the grill and enjoy with your favorite salsa!

## Nutrition:

Carbohydrates: 26.1 g

Protein: 9.2 g

Fat: 4.2 g

Sodium: 373.4 mg

Cholesterol: 19.8 mg

## 253. BBQ PULLED TUR-KEY SANDWICHES

|  Preparation Time: 30 minutes |  Cooking Time: 4 Hours |  Servings: 1 |
|---|---|---|

### Ingredients:

**6** skin-on turkey thighs

**6** split and buttered buns

**1 ½** cups of chicken broth

**1** cup of BBQ sauce

**Poultry** rub

### Directions:

**1.** Season the turkey thighs on both the sides with poultry rub

**2.** Set the grill to preheat by pushing the temperature to 180 degrees F

**3.** Arrange the turkey thighs on the grate of the grill and smoke it for 30 minutes

**4.** Now transfer the thighs to an aluminum foil which is disposable and then pour the brine right around the thighs

**5.** Cover it with a lid

**6.** Now increase the grill, temperature to 325 degrees F and roast the thigh till the internal temperature reaches 180 degrees F

**7.** Remove the foil from the grill but do not turn off the grill

**8.** Let the turkey thighs cool down a little

**9.** Now pour the dripping and serve

**10.** Remove the skin and discard it

**11.** Pull the meat into shreds and return it to the foil

**12.** Add 1 more cup of BBQ sauce and some more dripping

**13.** Now cover the foil with lid and re-heat the turkey on the smoker for half an hour

**14.** Serve and enjoy

### Nutrition:

Carbohydrates: 39 g

Protein: 29 g

Sodium: 15 mg

Cholesterol: 19 mg

## 254. THANKSGIVING TURKEY

|  Preparation Time: 15 minutes | Cooking Time: 4 hours | Servings: 6 |
|---|---|---|

### Ingredients:

**2** cups butter (softened)

**1** tablespoon cracked black pepper

**2** teaspoons kosher salt

**2** tablespoons freshly chopped rosemary

**2** tablespoons freshly chopped parsley

**2** tablespoons freshly chopped sage

**2** teaspoons dried thyme

**6** garlic cloves (minced)

**1** (18 pound) turkey

### Directions:

**1.** In a mixing bowl, combine the butter, sage, rosemary, 1 teaspoon black pepper, 1 teaspoon salt, thyme, parsley and garlic.

**2.** Use your fingers to loosen the skin from the turkey.

**3.** Generously, Rub butter mixture under the turkey skin and all over the turkey as well. 4. Season turkey generously with herb mix. 5. Preheat the grill to 300°F with lid closed for 15 minutes.

**4.** Place the turkey on the grill and roast for about 4 hours, or until the turkey thigh temperature reaches 160°F.

**5.** Take out the turkey meat from the grill and let it rest for a few minutes. Cut into sizes and serve.

### Nutrition:

Calories 278

Fat 30.8g

Carbs: 1.6g

Protein 0.6g

# 255. SMOKED TURKEY LEGS

|  |  |  |
|---|---|---|
| Preparation Time: 30 minutes | Cooking Time: 6 Hours | Servings: 1 |

## Ingredients:

4 turkey legs

2 bay leaves

1 cup of BBQ rubs

1 tablespoon of crushed allspice berries

2 teaspoons of liquid smoke

½ gal of cold water

4 cups of ice

1 gal of warm water

½ cup of brown sugar

½ cup of curing salt

1 tablespoon of peppercorns; whole black

## Directions:

**1.** Take a large stockpot and mix a gallon of warm water to curing salt, rub, peppercorns, brown sugar, liquid smoke, allspice and bay leaves

**2.** Bring this mix to boil by keeping the flame on high heat and let all salt granules dissolve thoroughly

**3.** Now let it cool to room temperature

**4.** Now add ice and cold water and let the whole thing chill in the refrigerator

**5.** Add turkey legs and make sure they are submerged in the brine

**6.** Let it stay for a day

**7.** Now drain the turkey legs and get rid of the brine

**8.** Wash off the brine from the legs with the help of cold water and then pat it dry

**9.** Set the grill to preheat by keeping the temperature to 250 degrees F

**10.** Lay the legs directly on the grate of the grill

**11.** Smoke it for 4 to 5 hours till the internal temperature reaches 165 degrees F

**12.** Serve and enjoy

## Nutrition:

Carbohydrates: 39 g

Protein: 29 g

Sodium: 15 mg

Cholesterol: 19 mg

# 256. SPATCHCOCK SMOKED TURKEY

| ⏲ | 🔥 | 👨‍🍳 |
|---|---|---|
| Preparation Time: 15 minutes | Cooking Time: 4 hours 3 minutes | Servings: 6 |

## Ingredients:

**1** (18 pounds) turkey

**2** tablespoons finely chopped fresh parsley

**1** tablespoon finely chopped fresh rosemary

**2** tablespoons finely chopped fresh thyme

**½** cup melted butter

**1** teaspoon garlic powder

**1** teaspoon onion powder

**1** teaspoon ground black pepper

**2** teaspoons salt or to taste

**2** tablespoons finely chopped scallions

## Directions:

**1.** Remove the turkey giblets and rinse turkey, in and out, under cold running water.

**2.** Place the turkey on a working surface, breast side down. Use a poultry shear to cut the turkey along both sides of the backbone to remove the turkey back bone.

**3.** Flip the turkey over, back side down. Now, press the turkey down to flatten it.

**4.** In a mixing bowl, combine the parsley, rosemary, scallions, thyme, butter, pepper, salt, and garlic and onion powder.

**5.** Rub butter mixture over all sides of the turkey.

**6.** Preheat your grill to HIGH (450°F) with lid closed for 15 minutes.

**7.** Place the turkey directly on the grill grate and cook for 30 minutes. Reduce the heat to 300°F and cook for an additional 4 hours, or until the internal temperature of the thickest part of the thigh reaches 165°F.

**8.** Take out the turkey meat from the grill and let it rest for a few minutes. Cut into sizes and serve.

## Nutrition:

Calories: 780
Fat: 19g
Carbs: 29.7g
Protein 116.4g

Chapter 5.

# POULTRY

# 257. BUFFALO CHICKEN WINGS

 Preparation
Time: 15 Minutes

 Cooking Time:
25 Minutes

 Servings:
6

**Ingredients:**

2 lb. chicken wings

1/2 cup sweet, spicy dry rub

2/3 cup buffalo sauce

**Celery,** chopped

**Directions:**

1. Start your wood pellet grill.

2. Set it to 450 degrees F.

3. Sprinkle the chicken wings with the dry rub.

4. Place on the grill rack.

5. Cook for 10 minutes per side.

6. Brush with the buffalo sauce.

7. Grill for another 5 minutes.

8. Dip each wing in the buffalo sauce.

9. Sprinkle the celery on top.

**Nutrition:**

Calories 935

Total fat 53g

Saturated fat 15g

Protein 107g

Sodium 320mg

# 258. SWEET AND SOUR CHICKEN

|  |  |  |
|---|---|---|
| Preparation Time: 30 Minutes | Cooking Time: 5 Hours | Servings: 4 |

## Ingredients:

**Eight** chicken drumsticks

**1/4** cup soy sauce

**1** cup ketchup

**Two** tablespoons rice wine vinegar

**Two** tablespoons lemon juice

**Two** tablespoons honey

**Two** tablespoons garlic, minced

**Two** tablespoons ginger, minced

**One** tablespoon sweet-spicy dry rub

**Three** tablespoons brown sugar

## Directions:

**1.** Combine all the sauce fixings in a bowl.

**2.** Mix well.

**3.** Take half of the mixture, transfer to another bowl and refrigerate.

**4.** Add the chicken to the bowl with the remaining sauce.

**5.** Toss to coat evenly.

**6.** Cover and refrigerate for 4 hours.

**7.** When ready to cook, take the chicken out of the refrigerator.

**8.** Discard the marinade.

**9.** Turn on your wood pellet grill.

**10.** Set it to smoke.

**11.** Set the temperature to 225 degrees F.

**12.** Smoke the chicken for 3 hours.

**13.** Serve the chicken with the reserved sauce.

## Nutrition:

Calories 935

Total fat 53g

Saturated fat 15g

Protein 107g

Sodium 320mg

# 259. HONEY GLAZED WHOLE CHICKEN

|  | |  |
|---|---|---|
| Preparation Time: 30 Minutes | Cooking Time: 4 Hours | Servings: 4 |

## Ingredients:

**One** tablespoon honey

**Four** tablespoons butter

**Three** tablespoons lemon juice

**One** whole chicken, giblets trimmed

**Four** tablespoons chicken seasoning

## Directions:

**1.** Set your wood pellet grill to smoke.

**2.** Set it to 225 degrees F.

**3.** In a pan over low heat, increase the honey and butter. Pour in the lemon juice.

**4.** Add the seasoning.

**5.** Cook for 1 minute, stirring.

**6.** Add the chicken to the grill.

**7.** Smoke for 8 minutes.

**8.** Flip the chicken and brush with the honey mixture.

**9.** Smoke for 3 hours, brushing the sauce every 40 minutes.

**10.** Let rest for 5 minutes before serving.

## Nutrition:

Calories 935

Total fat 53g

Saturated fat 15g

Protein 107g

Sodium 320mg

## 260. CHICKEN LOLLIPOPS

🕐 Preparation Time: 30 Minutes

🔥 Cooking Time: 2 Hours

👨‍🍳 Servings: 6

### Ingredients:

**12** chicken lollipops

**Chicken** seasoning

**Ten** tablespoons butter, sliced into 12 cubes

**1** cup barbecue sauce

**1** cup hot sauce

### Directions:

**1.** Turn on your wood pellet grill.

**2.** Set it to 300 degrees F.

**3.** Then season, the chicken with the chicken seasoning.

**4.** Arrange the chicken in a baking pan.

**5.** Put the butter cubes on top of each chicken.

**6.** Cook the chicken lollipops for 2 hours, basting with the melted butter in the baking pan every 20 minutes.

**7.** Pour in the barbecue sauce and hot sauce over the chicken.

**8.** Grill for 15 minutes.

### Nutrition:

Calories 935

Total fat 53g

Saturated fat 15g

Protein 107g

Sodium 320mg

## 261. LEMON CHICKEN IN FOIL PACKET

🕐 Preparation Time: 5 Minutes

🔥 Cooking Time: 25 Minutes

👨‍🍳 Servings: 4

### Ingredients:

**Four** chicken fillets

**Three** tablespoons melted butter

**One** garlic, minced

**1-1/2** teaspoon dried Italian seasoning

**Salt** and pepper to taste

**One** lemon, sliced

### Directions:

**1.** Turn on your wood pellet grill.

**2.** Keep the lid open while burning for 5 minutes.

**3.** Preheat it to 450 degrees F.

**4.** Add the chicken fillet on top of foil sheets.

**5.** In a bowl, mix the butter, garlic, seasoning, salt, and pepper.

**6.** Brush the chicken with this mixture.

**7.** Put the lemon slices on top.

**8.** Wrap the chicken with the foil.

**9.** Grill each side for 7 to 10 minutes per side.

### Nutrition:

Calories 935

Total fat 53g

Saturated fat 15g

Protein 107g

Sodium 320mg

# 262. ASIAN WINGS

Preparation
Time: 30 Minutes

Cooking Time:
3 Hours

Servings:
6

## Ingredients:

**One** teaspoon honey

**One** teaspoon soy sauce

**Two** teaspoon rice vinegar

**1/2** cup hoisin sauce

**Two** teaspoon sesame oil

**One** teaspoon ginger, minced

**One** teaspoon garlic, minced

**One** teaspoon green onion, chopped

**1** cup hot water

**2** lb. chicken wings

## Directions:

1. Combine all the sauce fixings in a large bowl. Mix well.

2. Transfer 1/3 of the sauce to another bowl and refrigerate.

3. Add the chicken wings to the remaining sauce.

4. Cover and refrigerate for 2 hours.

5. Turn on your wood pellet grill.

6. Set it to 300 degrees F.

7. Add the wings to a grilling basket.

8. Cook for 1 hour.

9. Heat the reserved sauce in a pan.

10. Bring to a boil and then simmer for 10 minutes.

11. Brush the chicken with the remaining sauce.

12. Grill for another 10 minutes.

13. Let rest for 5 minutes before serving.

## Nutrition:

Calories 935

Total fat 53g

Saturated fat 15g

Protein 107g

Sodium 320mg

# 263. SWEET AND SPICY CHICKEN

|  Preparation Time: 30 Minutes |  Cooking Time: 1 H + 30 Minutes | Servings: 4 |

## Ingredients:

**16** chicken wings

**Three** tablespoons lime juice

**A** sweet, spicy rub

## Directions:

**1.** Arrange the chicken wings in a baking pan.

**2.** Pour the lime juice over the wings.

**3.** Sprinkle the wings with the seasoning.

**4.** Set your wood pellet grill to 350 degrees F.

**5.** Add the chicken wings to the grill.

**6.** Grill for 20 minutes per side.

## Nutrition:

Calories 935

Total fat 53g

Saturated fat 15g

Protein 107g

Sodium 320mg

---

# 264. TERIYAKI TURKEY

|  Preparation Time: 30 Minutes |  Cooking Time: 4 Hours |  Servings: 10 |

## Ingredients:

**Glaze**

**1/4** cup melted butter

**1/2** cup apple cider

**Two** cloves garlic, minced

**1/2** teaspoon ground ginger

**Two** tablespoons soy sauce

**Two** tablespoons honey

**Turkey**

**Two** tablespoons chicken seasoning

**One** whole turkey

**Thickener**

**One** tablespoon cold water

**One** teaspoon cornstarch

## Directions:

**1.** Add the glaze ingredients to a pan over medium heat.

**2.** Bring to a boil and then simmer for 5 minutes.

**3.** Reserve 5 tablespoons of the mixture.

**4.** Add the remaining to a marinade injection.

**5.** Place the turkey in a baking pan.

**6.** Season with the chicken seasoning.

**7.** Turn on the wood pellet grill.

**8.** Set it to 300 degrees F.

**9.** Add the turkey to the grill.

**10.** Cook for 3 hours.

**11.** Add the thickener to the reserved mixture.

**12.** Brush the turkey with this sauce.

**13.** Cook for another 1 hour.

## Nutrition:

Calories 935

Total fat 53g

Saturated fat 15g

Protein 107g

Sodium 320mg

## 265. CHEESY TURKEY BURGER

| ⏱ Preparation Time: 20 Minutes | 🔥 Cooking Time: 3 Hours | 👨‍🍳 Servings: 8 |
|---|---|---|

**Ingredients:**

**3** lb. ground turkey

**Burger** seasoning

**7** oz. brie cheese, sliced into cubes

**Eight** burger buns, sliced

**Blueberry** jam

**Two** roasted bell peppers, sliced

**Directions:**

**1.** Season the turkey with the burger seasoning.

**2.** Mix well.

**3.** Form 8 patties from the mixture.

**4.** Press cheese into the patties.

**5.** Cover the top with more turkey.

**6.** Preheat your wood pellet grill to 350 degrees F.

**7.** Cook the turkey burgers for 30 to 40 minutes per side.

**8.** Spread the burger buns with blueberry jam.

**9.** Add the turkey burger on top.

**10.** Top with the bell peppers.

**Nutrition:**

Calories 935

Total fat 53g

Saturated fat 15g

Protein 107g

Sodium 320mg

## 266. TURKEY SANDWICH

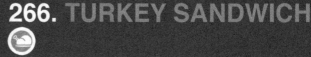

| ⏱ Preparation Time: 5 Minutes | 🔥 Cooking Time: 25 Minutes | 👨‍🍳 Servings: 4 |
|---|---|---|

**Ingredients:**

**Eight** bread slices

**1** cup gravy

**2** cups turkey, cooked and shredded

**Directions:**

**1.** Set your wood pellet grill to smoke.

**2.** Preheat it to 400 degrees F.

**3.** Place a grill mat on top of the grates.

**4.** Add the turkey on top of the mat.

**5.** Cook for 10 minutes.

**6.** Toast the bread in the flame broiler.

**7.** Top the bread with the gravy and shredded turkey.

**Nutrition:**

Calories 935

Total fat 53g

Saturated fat 15g

Protein 107g

Sodium 320mg

## 267. SMOKED TURKEY

|  |  |  |
|---|---|---|
| Preparation Time: 30 Minutes | Cooking Time: 6 H + 30 Minutes | Servings: 8 |

**Ingredients:**

**1** cup butter

**1/2** cup maple syrup

**Two** tablespoons chicken seasoning

**One** whole turkey

**Directions:**

**1.** Add the butter to a pan over low heat.

**2.** Stir in the maple syrup.

**3.** Simmer for 5 minutes, stirring.

**4.** Turn off the stove and let cool.

**5.** Add to a marinade injection.

**6.** Inject into the turkey.

**7.** Add the turkey to the wood pellet grill.

**8.** Set it smoke.

**9.** Smoke at 275 degrees F for 6 hours.

## 268. TEXAS TURKEY

|  |  |  |
|---|---|---|
| Preparation Time: 30 Minutes | Cooking Time: 4 H + 30 Minutes | Servings: 8 |

**Ingredients:**

**One** pre-brined turkey

**Salt** and pepper to taste

**1** lb. butter

**Directions:**

**1.** Preheat your wood pellet grill to 300 degrees F.

**2.** Season the turkey with salt and pepper.

**3.** Grill for 3 hours.

**4.** Add the turkey to a roasting pan.

**5.** Cover the turkey with the butter.

**6.** Cover with foil.

**7.** Add to the grill and cook for another 1 hour.

**8.** Let rest for 20 minutes before carving and serving.

**Nutrition:**

Calories 935

Total fat 53g

Saturated fat 15g

Protein 107g

Sodium 320mg

**Nutrition:**

Calories 935

Total fat 53g

Saturated fat 15g

Protein 107g

Sodium 320mg

## 269. TRAEGER GRILLED CHICKEN

|  |  |  |
|---|---|---|
| Preparation Time: 10 Minutes | Cooking Time: 1 H + 10 Minutes | Servings: 6 |

**Ingredients:**

**5** lb. whole chicken

**1/2** cup oil

**Traeger** chicken rub

**Directions:**

**1.** Preheat the Traeger on the smoke setting with the lid open for 5 minutes. Close the lid, and let it warm for 15 minutes or until it reaches 450.

**2.** Use bakers' twine to tie the chicken legs together, then rub it with oil. Coat the chicken with the rub and place it on the grill.

**3.** Grill for 70 minutes with the lid closed or until it reaches an internal temperature of 1650F.

**4.** Remove the chicken from the Traeger and let rest for 15 minutes. Cut and serve.

**Nutrition:**

Calories 935

Total fat 53g

Saturated fat 15g

Protein 107g

Sodium 320mg

## 270. TRAGER SMOKED SPATCHCOCK TURKEY

| Preparation Time: 30 Minutes | Cooking Time: 1 H + 15 Minutes | Servings: 8 |
|---|---|---|

**Ingredients:**

**One** turkey

**1/2** cup melted butter

**1/4** cup Traeger chicken rub

**1** tbsp onion powder

**1** tbsp garlic powder

**1** tbsp rubbed sage

**Directions:**

**1.** Preheat your Traeger to high temperature.

**2.** Put the turkey on a chopping board with the breast side down and the legs pointing towards you.

**3.** Cut either side of the turkey backbone to remove the spine. Flip the turkey and place it on a pan

**4.** Season both sides with the seasonings and place it on the grill skin side up on the grill.

**5.** Cook for 30 minutes, reduce temperature, and cook for 45 more minutes until the internal temperature reaches 1650F.

**6.** Remove from the Traeger and let rest for 15 minutes before slicing and serving.

**Nutrition:**

Calories 156

Total fat 16g

Saturated fat 2g

Total carbs 1g

Net carbs 1g

Protein 2g

Sodium 19mg

# 271. GRILLED CHILE LIME CHICKEN

| Preparation Time: 10 minutes | Cooking Time: 10 minutes | Servings: 4 |

## Ingredients:

**One-fourth** cup fresh lime juice

**One** lime, zested

**One** teaspoon red pepper flake

**Half** teaspoon ground cumin

**One** teaspoon salt

**One** teaspoon brown sugar

**Four** medium skinless, boneless chicken breast halves

**Two** tablespoons chopped fresh cilantro

**Two** tablespoons olive oil

**Two** cloves garlic, minced

## Directions:

**1.** First, take a little bowl and whisk lime juice, lime zest, cumin, olive oil, brown sugar, garlic, salt, and red pepper flakes. Add chicken in the bowl or big plastic bag and then add the lime marinade. Seal the bag and wrap the bowl and keep in the freezer to preserve for a half-hour to one day.

**2.** Now, preheat grill middle to high heat and lightly oil the grate.

**3.** Add chicken breasts on the preheated grill and fry until it gets pink in the middle and skin gets golden and lightly charred for five minutes per side.

**4.** Move chicken breast to the plate and allow stand for five minutes and cut and decorate with cilantro.

**5.** Additional Tip

**6.** Make sure that before adding chicken, reserve it, and avoid contamination.

## Nutrition:

Energy (calories): 48 kcal

Protein: 0.48 g

Fat: 3.54 g

Carbohydrates: 4.88 g

# 272. TRAEGER CHICKEN BREAST

| Preparation Time: 10 Minutes | Cooking Time: 15 Minutes | Servings: 6 |

## Ingredients:

**Three** chicken breasts

**1** tbsp avocado oil

**1/4** tbsp garlic powder

**1/4** tbsp onion powder

**3/4** tbsp salt

**1/4** tbsp pepper

## Directions:

**1.** Preheat your Traeger to 3750F

**2.** Cut the chicken breast into halves lengthwise, then coat with avocado oil.

**3.** Season with garlic powder, onion powder, salt, and pepper.

**4.** Place the chicken on the grill and cook for 7 minutes on each side or until the internal temperature reaches 1650F

## Nutrition:

Calories 120

Total fat 4g

Saturated fat 1g

Protein 19g

Sodium 309mg

# 273. TASTY CHICKEN SATAY

Preparation time: 25 minutes

Cooking time: 20 minutes

Servings: 20

## Ingredients

**Twenty** wooden skewers

**Six** boneless, skinless chicken breasts, cut lengthwise into strips

**Marinade:**

**six** tablespoons soy sauce

**six** tablespoons tomato sauce

**two** tablespoons peanut oil

**four** cloves garlic, minced

**half** teaspoon ground black pepper

**half** teaspoon ground cumin

**Peanut** Sauce:

**one** tablespoon peanut oil

**one-fourth** onion, finely chopped

**one** clove garlic, minced

**eight** tablespoons peanut butter

**three** tablespoons white sugar

**two** tablespoons soy sauce

**one** cup of water

**Half** lemon, juiced

## Directions:

**1.** Place wooden skewers in the deep dish and wrap with water and allow soaking for twenty minutes.

**2.** Take bowls add chicken strips and merge tomato sauce, peanut oil, soy sauce, cumin, pepper, and garlic in the little bowl and merge to combine.

**3.** Pour chicken strips and merge chicken is coated well on each side.

**4.** Marinate for fifteen minutes.

**5.** Now, form peanut sauce. After this, add one tablespoon oil in the warm skillet over the intermediate to high heat. Add garlic and onion and cook it well. Stir until onion gets translucent and soft for four minutes.

**6.** Now, add soy sauce, butter, water, and sugar and merge well. Cook well until the sauce gets thicken slowly for five minutes. Add in the juice of a lemon and eliminate it from the flame.

**7.** After this, preheat a grill for elevated heat and then lightly oil the grate. Thread every chicken strip on the skewer.

**8.** Keep skewers on the preheated grill and fry for ten minutes and flipping through cooking. Serve the satay skewers instantly with peanut sauce.

## Nutrition:

Energy (calories): 109 kcal

Protein: 1.28 g

Fat: 9.18 g

Carbohydrates: 5.89 g

## 274. EASY GRILLED CHICKEN

| Preparation Time: 10 minutes | Cooking Time: 35 minutes | Servings: 12 |
|---|---|---|

### Ingredients

**Two** cups white distilled vinegar

**Two** cups of water

**Two** sticks butter

**Four** tablespoons Worcestershire sauce

**Two** teaspoons minced garlic

**Two** bone-in chicken breasts

**Four** medium chicken leg quarters

**Four** tablespoons garlic salt

**Two** tablespoons ground black pepper

**One** tablespoon white sugar

### Directions:

**1.** Merge Worcestershire sauce, water, vinegar, butter, minced garlic, garlic salt, sugar in the pot and boil it. Eliminate from the flame and allow the marinade to cool at room temperature approximately half-hour.

**2.** Add chicken in the plastic bag and pour marinade over the chicken and seal it and then preserve it for eight to the whole night.

**3.** After, preheat the grill for intermediate to elevate heat lightly oil the grate.

**4.** Move chicken pieces to the grill and stir it well, remove the marinade

**5.** Grill chicken until it gets pink in the middle for thirty to forty-five minutes. The thermometer is inserted in the bone temperature reaches 165F.

### Nutrition:

Energy (calories): 74 kcal

Protein: 7.56 g

Fat: 2.13 g

Carbohydrates: 3.48 g

## 275. CHICKEN WITH LEMON YOGURT

| Preparation Time: 15 minutes | Cooking Time: 35 minutes | Servings: 6 |
|---|---|---|

### Ingredients

**Half** cup plain low-fat Greek yogurt

**Half** lemon, juiced

**One** tablespoon lemon zest

**One** teaspoon herb de Provence

**One** teaspoon salt

**One** teaspoon ground black pepper

**one** whole chicken, cut into eight pieces

**One** tablespoon olive oil

**Four** cloves garlic,

**One** tablespoon paprika

**Half** cup plain low-fat Greek yogurt

**One** tablespoon lemon juice

**One** teaspoon harissa

**One** pinch salt

### Directions:

**1.** Mix the yogurt, lemon juice, and zest.

**2.** Pour the mixture into a large zip-top bag. Close the bag and make sure the chicken is completely covered in the yogurt flavor.

**3.** In a bowl, mix the herb de Provence, salt, black pepper, oil, and garlic

**4.** Add the chicken to the bowl. Close the bag tight and move the chicken around so it is completely coated in the mixture.

**5.** In a separate bowl, mix the paprika, lemon juice, yogurt, harissa, and a pinch of salt.

**6.** Store the bowls in the fridge for two hours.

**7.** While the chicken sits in the marinades, preheat the oven to 425 degrees and bake the chicken for one hour.

**8.** Pour the sauce into a large skillet and let it simmer for three minutes. Place the chicken in the sauce for three minutes.

### Nutrition:

Energy (calories): 245 kcal

Protein: 14.07 g

Fat: 11.15 g

Carbohydrates: 24.97 g

# 276. CHICKEN THIGHS WITH SALSA

 Preparation
Time: 15 minutes

 Cooking Time:
10 minutes

 Servings:
8

## Ingredients

**Marinade**

**One-fourth** cup extra-virgin olive oil

**one** orange, juiced

**half** teaspoon ground cumin

**One-fourth** teaspoon ground coriander

**One-fourth** teaspoon cayenne pepper

**One-fourth** teaspoon smoked paprika

**one** lime, juiced

**two** cloves garlic, minced

**One** pinch salt and ground black pepper

**Eight** thighs, bone, and skin removed skinless and boneless chicken thighs

**Salsa**

**One** and half cups diced and peeled fresh peaches

**One** cup pitted and diced red cherries

**One-third** cup chopped cilantro

**One** tablespoon fresh lime juice

**Two** tablespoons extra-virgin olive oil

**Two** tablespoons seeded and minced jalapeno pepper

**Two** tablespoons minced red onion

## Directions:

**1.** Preheat the oven to 425 degrees Fahrenheit. Cover a baking sheet with foil.

**2.** To make the marinade, in a blender, blend together the olive oil, orange juice, cumin, coriander, cayenne, smoked paprika, lime juice, garlic, and salt, and black pepper until well blended. Spread the chicken in a baking dish and pour the marinade all over it to coat. Refrigerate the chicken for at least 30 minutes.

**3.** To make the salsa, in a large bowl, combine the peaches, cherries, cilantro, lime juice, olive oil, jalapeno, and onion. Season with salt and pepper.

**4.** Combine the chicken thighs in the baking dish with the salsa. Cover the dish with foil and roast for 35 minutes.

**5.** Remove the cover and continue roasting for another 10 minutes, or until opaque and no longer pink.

**6.** Serve with a side of cilantro black beans and corn.

## Nutrition:

Energy (calories): 589 kcal
Protein: 22.41 g
Fat: 44.83 g
Carbohydrates: 25.42 g

## 277. CHICKEN THIGH KEBABS WITH LIME

|  |  |  |
|---|---|---|
| Preparation Time: 20 minutes | Cooking Time: 15 minutes | Servings: 4 |

### Ingredients

**Glaze:**

**One-fourth** cup honey

**One** tablespoon lime juice

**Two** tablespoons Sriracha sauce

**Kebabs:**

**Eight** large metal skewers

**One** pound boneless and skinless chicken thighs

**Half** small fresh pineapples

**one** medium red onion,

**One** red sweet pepper

**One** medium zucchini

**two** tablespoons olive oil

**one** pinch salt and freshly ground black pepper

**one** pinch garlic powder,

**one** teaspoon lime zest

### Directions:

**1.** Prepare the glaze by whisking the ingredients together. Set the marinade aside.

**2.** Skewer the chicken thighs with onions, peppers, pineapples, and zucchini. Use alternating pieces of each vegetable for a balanced kebab. Use one-third of the chicken for each kebab. Season to taste.

**3.** Set the kebabs in a grill and cook over medium-high heat for about 3 to 4 minutes, rotating to prevent the chicken from burning.

**4.** Apply the glaze before serving. Enjoy!

**Nutrition:**

Energy (calories): 251 kcal
Protein: 26.22 g
Fat: 6.55 g
Carbohydrates: 22.03 g

## 278. CILANTRO GRILLED CHICKEN

|  | |  |
|---|---|---|
| Preparation Time: 15 minutes | Cooking Time: 30 minutes | Servings: 6 |

### Ingredients

**Four** limes juiced

**Half** cup chopped fresh cilantro

**Two** tablespoons ground black pepper

**One** whole chicken

**Two** tablespoons garlic salt

### Directions:

**1.** Grill the whole chicken on medium-high until the inside temperature reaches 160 degrees Fahrenheit, stopping every five minutes to reapply cilantro, lime juice, and pepper.

**2.** Let the chicken cool before eating, and enjoy"

**Nutrition:**

Energy (calories): 583 kcal
Protein: 98.77 g
Fat: 13.25 g
Carbohydrates: 14.93 g
Fiber: .5 g

## 279. TASTY THAI CHICKEN SATAY

| Preparation Time: 20 minu-tes | Cooking Time: 20 minutes | Servings: 8 |
|---|---|---|

### Ingredients

**2** tablespoons vegetable oil

**2** tablespoons soy sauce

**1** teaspoon ground cumin

**1** teaspoon ground coriander

**2** pounds skinless, boneless chicken breast

**20** reaches wooden skewers

**2** tablespoons crunchy peanut butter

**2** tablespoons chopped peanuts

**1** tablespoon lime juice

**1** teaspoon muscovado sugar

**2** teaspoons tamarind paste

**1** stalk lemongrass

**2cloves** garlic

**Half** teaspoon chili powder

**1** can coconut milk

**2** teaspoons red Thai curry paste

**1** tablespoon fish sauce

**1** teaspoon tomato paste

**1** tablespoon brown sugar

### Directions:

**1.** Preheat the oven to 180C. Grease a shallow baking tray with oil.

**2.** Put the chicken in a bowl and whisk in 2 tablespoons vegetable oil, the soy sauce, cumin, coriander, half the peanut butter, half the peanuts, half the lime juice, the muscovado sugar, tamarind paste, sliced lemongrass, minced garlic, chili powder and a quarter teaspoon of salt, then mix thoroughly.

**3.** Thread the chicken onto the skewers. Push the skewers down onto the baking tray, brush the chicken with the remaining marinade and then bake for 20 minutes. While the chicken is cooking, mix the remaining ingredients in a saucepan with 1/2 cup water over medium heat for about 5 minutes.

**4.** Remove the skewers, cool, and serve with sauce.

### Nutrition:

Energy (calories): 234 kcal

Protein: 28.22 g; Fat: 9.63 g

Carbohydrates: 7.97 g

## 280. QUICK ROTISSERIE CHICKEN

| Preparation time: 15 minutes | Cooking time: 1 hour 30 minutes | Servings: 6 |
|---|---|---|

### Ingredients

**1** whole chicken

**1** pinch salt

**One-fourth** cup butter, melted

**One-fourth** tablespoon ground black pepper

**1** tablespoon salt

**1** tablespoon paprika

### Directions:

**1.** First, season the inner side of the chicken with a pinch of salt and put the chicken on to rotisserie and arrange the grill on high. Cook it well for ten minutes.

**2.** During this, rapidly merge the paprika, one tablespoon salt, butter, and pepper and then turn the grill down to intermediate and baste the chicken with a mixture of butter.

**3.** Seal the lid and cook for one to one and a half hours and then basting infrequently until inner temperature reaches 180 degrees.

**4.** Eliminate from the rotisserie and allow standing for ten to fifteen minutes before slicing into pieces and serve.

### Nutrition:

Energy (calories): 454 kcal

Protein: 32.96 g

Fat: 35.14 g

Carbohydrates: 1.34 g

## 281. GRILLED CHICKEN MARINADE

| | | |
|---|---|---|
| Preparation time: 10 minutes | Cooking time 10 minutes | Servings: 5 |

### Ingredients

**1/4** cup red wine vinegar

**1** and a half teaspoons dried parsley flakes

**Half** teaspoon dried basil

**Half** teaspoon dried oregano

**One-fourth** teaspoon garlic powder

**One-fourth** teaspoon ground black pepper

**One-fourth** cup reduced-sodium soy sauce

**One-fourth** cup olive oil

**5** boneless and skinless chicken breasts

### Directions:

**1.** First, whisk the olive oil, oregano, soy sauce, parsley, vinegar, garlic powder, basil, and black pepper in the bowl. Now, pour this in the plastic bag. Now add the chicken in it and coat with marinade and squeeze out the extra air and close the bag.

**2.** Marinade in the freezer at least four hours.

**3.** After this, preheat the grill for middle to low heat and then lightly oil grate. Drain it and remove marinade.

**4.** After, grill the chicken on the preheated grill until it gets no longer pink in the middle for four to five minutes each side. Take instant-read thermometer and then inserted in the middle. The thermometer should read at least 165 degrees.

### Nutrition:

Energy (calories): 107 kcal

Protein: 1.29 g

Fat: 10.86 g

Carbohydrates: 1.29g

## 282. SMOKEY PEPPERED BACON CHICKEN ON A STICK

| | | |
|---|---|---|
| Preparation Time: 15 minutes | Cooking Time: 10 minutes | Servings: 6 |

### Ingredients:

**1 1/2 pounds** boneless chicken breasts, cubed

**1/2-pound** peppered bacon, chopped

**1/4** cup apple cider vinegar

**4** cloves garlic

**1/4** cup brown sugar

**3** tablespoons smoked paprika

**1** teaspoon salt

**1** teaspoon coarse ground black pepper

**1 1/2** cups smoke and tang sauce

### Directions:

**1.** Combine chicken, bacon, vinegar, and garlic in a slow cooker.

**2.** In a medium bowl, whisk together the remaining ingredients.

**3.** Stir into the slow cooker.

**4.** Cover, and bake on high for 10 minutes.

**5.** Then serve.

### Nutrition:

Energy (calories): 362 kcal

Protein: 29.29 g

Fat: 22.21 g

Carbohydrates: 13.5 g

## 283. SLOW COOKED SMOLDERING SHREDDED CHICKEN

|  |  |  |
|---|---|---|
| Preparation Time: 10 minutes | Cooking Time: 6 hours | Servings: 6-8 |

### Ingredients:

**2** pounds boneless skinless chicken breast

**One-half** teaspoon salt

**One-half** teaspoon black pepper

**1** cup BBQ sauce of choice

**One-fourth** cup apple cider vinegar

**One-fourth** cup brown sugar

**1** tablespoon liquid smoke

**2** jalapeno peppers, seeded and minced

**4** cloves garlic, crushed and minced

### Directions:

**1.** Season the chicken with the salt and black pepper and then place it in a slow cooker.

**2.** In a bowl, combine the BBQ sauce, apple cider vinegar, brown sugar, liquid smoke, jalapeno peppers and garlic. Whisk until well combined.

**3.** Pour the sauce over the chicken, cover and cook on low for 6 hours.

**4.** A few minutes before you are ready to remove the cover from the slow cooker, preheat an outdoor or indoor grill over medium high heat.

**5.** Remove the chicken breasts from the slow cooker and place them on the grill just long enough for light caramelization to occur.

**6.** Place each chicken breast on a cutting board and, using two forks, shred it and place it back into the slow cooker.

**7.** Toss the chicken with the sauce and serve.

### Nutrition:

Energy (calories): 284 kcal

Protein: 34.97 g

Fat: 4.12 g

Carbohydrates: 25.53 g

## 284. CLUCKY KENTUCKY HOT BROWN CASSEROLE

|  |  |  |
|---|---|---|
| Preparation Time: 10 minutes | Cooking Time: 40 minutes | Servings: 8-10 |

### Ingredients:

**One-fourth** cup butter

**One-fourth** cup flour

**4** cups milk

**1** egg

**1** cup fresh grated parmesan cheese

**One-half** teaspoon salt

**1** teaspoon coarse ground black pepper

**1** teaspoon granulated garlic

**1** teaspoon smoked paprika

**12** slices white or sourdough bread, toasted and cubed

**1½** pounds cooked, smoked chicken, either shredded or sliced thin

**½** pound bacon

**1** cup heirloom tomato, sliced

**½** cup parmesan cheese

**¼** cup fresh parsley, chopped

### Directions:

**1.** Preheat oven to 350F.

**2.** Heat ¼ cup butter in a large pot over medium-high heat.

**3.** Add flour and cook until lightly browned about 1-2 minutes.

**4.** Whisk in milk and simmer until thickened, about 8 minutes.

**5.** Whisk in remaining ingredients, except chicken, bacon, tomato, parsley, and parmesan cheese.

**6.** Simmer mixture, stirring occasionally, until it thickens, about 5-7 minutes.

**7.** Add chicken, bacon, and tomatoes.

**8.** Remove from heat.

**9.** Pour mixture into a greased 9x13" casserole dish.

**10.** Top with parmesan cheese and parsley.

**11.** Bake uncovered in the preheated oven until golden brown, about 40 minutes.

**12.** Serve hot.

### Nutrition:

Energy (calories): 691 kcal

Protein: 29.03 g

Fat: 48.9 g

Carbohydrates: 34.64 g

## 285. VINEGAR MOP'D HEIRLOOM TOMATO AND CHICKEN TOSS

|  |  |  |
|---|---|---|
| Preparation Time: 10 minutes | Cooking Time: 10 minutes | Servings: 4 |

### Ingredients:

**1-pound** boneless skinless chicken breast, sliced thin

**4** cups assorted heirloom tomatoes, cut into thick wedges

**1** cup onion, cut into wedges

**1½** cups apple cider vinegar

**1** tablespoon sorghum molasses

**1** tablespoon Dijon mustard

**2** teaspoons crushed red pepper flakes

**½** teaspoon salt

### Directions:

**1.** Combine the chicken breasts, heirloom tomatoes and onions together in a large bowl.

**2.** In a smaller bowl, whisk together the apple cider vinegar, sorghum molasses, Dijon mustard, crushed red pepper flakes and salt.

**3.** Pour the mixture over the chicken and tomatoes. Toss to mix.

**4.** Cover and refrigerate for at least 2 hours.

**5.** Remove the bowl from the refrigerator and let it sit out for 15 minutes.

**6.** Meanwhile, prepare an indoor or outdoor grill over medium heat.

**7.** Remove the chicken, tomatoes and onions from the marinade and set aside. Keep remaining marinade. Add marinade to a small saucepan and bring to a boil. Set aside.

**8.** If the spaces on your grill grate are large enough for the chicken or vegetables to fall through, line the grill with a piece of aluminum foil. Add chicken and tomatoes to the grill.

**9.** Grill for 10 minutes, turning occasionally, until the chicken is cooked through.

**10.** Use the marinade as a mop while grilling, if desired.

### Nutrition:

Energy (calories): 227 kcal
Protein: 27.56 g
Fat: 3.62 g
Carbohydrates: 20.77 g

## 286. BLUEGRASS CHICKEN SALAD

| |  | |
|---|---|---|
| Preparation Time: 15 minutes | Cooking Time: 5 minutes | Servings: 4 |

### Ingredients:

**½** cup walnut oil

**¼** cup apple cider vinegar

**1** tablespoon red wine vinegar

**1** tablespoon brown sugar

**1** tablespoon butter

**¼** cup walnuts, chopped

**2** tablespoons Kentucky bourbon

**4** cups fresh arugula

**4** cups fresh spinach, torn

**1** cup white asparagus tips, lightly steamed

**1** cup blackberries, halved

**½** cup gorgonzola cheese

**1-pound** smoked chicken, shredded or sliced, preferably warm

### Directions:

**1.** In a bowl, whisk together the walnut oil, apple cider vinegar, red wine vinegar and brown sugar until completely blended. Cover and refrigerate for at least 1 hour.

**2.** Melt the butter in a small skillet over medium heat.

**3.** Once the butter has melted, add the walnuts and stir.

**4.** Cook the walnuts for 2–3 minutes.

**5.** Add the bourbon to the skillet and cook, stirring frequently, until the bourbon reduces.

**6.** Combine the arugula and spinach.

**7.** Drizzle the dressing over the greens to taste, tossing the salad as you go.

**8.** Add the white asparagus, blackberries and gorgonzola cheese to the bowl. Toss gently.

**9.** Distribute the salad among serving plates.

**10.** Top each portion with warmed smoked chicken and bourbon walnuts before serving.

### Nutrition:

Energy (calories): 967 kcal
Protein: 30.46 g
Fat: 84.77 g
Carbohydrates: 22.74 g

# 287. KENTUCKY SMOKED WHOLE CHICKEN

|  |  | 🎩 |
|---|---|---|
| Preparation Time: 10 minutes | Cooking Time: 2 hours | Servings: 4-6 |

## Ingredients:

**1** whole chicken, approximately 3–4 pounds

**2** quarts purified water

**One-fourth** cup kosher salt

**One-fourth** cup Kentucky bourbon

**2** tablespoons molasses

**One-fourth** cup brown sugar

**One-fourth** cup apple cider vinegar

**1** tablespoon pink peppercorns

**4** bay leaves

**1** tablespoon fresh grated ginger

**4** cloves garlic

**1** cup Vidalia onion, sliced thick

**1** cup apple, cut into wedges

**1** cup orange wedges

**1** tablespoon butter, melted

**4** cups ice

**Woodchips** of choice for smoking

## Directions:

**1.** Trim excess fat off of chicken and wash inside and out with hot water. Pat chicken dry with paper towels. Season inside cavity with salt. Place chicken over a bed of ice and refrigerate until ready to cook.

**2.** Place them in a pan. Add water and remaining ingredients except for ice and woodchips. Cook chicken in water for 2 hours at a simmer (if not using a smoker). Allow chicken to cool in liquid in the refrigerator.

**3.** Remove chicken from cooker and place on a preheated smoker. Use woodchips of choice (hickory, apple, cherry, etc.) to smoke the chicken for 30-45 minutes (taste one every 10 minutes until you find the perfect flavor).

**4.** Remove chicken from the cooker and discard liquid. Allow resting 15-20 minutes before carving. Paint your finished product with butter and garnishing of thinly sliced Vidalia onion.

## Nutrition:

Energy (calories): 518 kcal

Protein: 50.33 g

Fat: 9.65 g

Carbohydrates: 56.21 g

# 288. CHICKEN BOMBS STUFFED WITH KENTUCKY FRIED CORN

| 🕐 | 🔥 | 👨‍🍳 |
|---|---|---|
| Preparation Time: 15 minutes | Cooking Time: 45 minutes | Servings: 6 |

## Ingredients:

1½ pounds boneless, skinless chicken breasts

½ teaspoon salt

1 teaspoon coarse ground black pepper

**1-pound** hickory smoked bacon, thin sliced

2 cups fresh corn kernels

1 cup green bell pepper, chopped

½ cup red onion, chopped

1 egg, lightly beaten

½ cup cream cheese

1 teaspoon cayenne sauce

1 cup basting sauce of choice

## Directions:

**1.** Preheat oven to 350 degrees F. Spray baking sheets with nonstick cooking spray. Place chicken in a large, resealable plastic bag. Season with salt and pepper.

**2.** Pour in the bacon and shake to coat. Place in a single layer on baking sheets. Bake for 40 minutes or until chicken is thoroughly cooked and tender.

**3.** Remove from oven and allow to cool. Shred chicken and toss with corn, bell pepper, and onion in a medium bowl. Place mixture in the middle of a chicken breast; roll up and secure with a toothpick. Lightly grease a large skillet with a small amount of oil and bring to medium-high heat. Add egg and cream cheese to a bowl and mix with a fork until blended.

**4.** Place ½ cup of filling near the end. Roll up and secure with a toothpick, then dip in egg and cheese mixture. Place on a plate and repeat until all of the fillings are used. Heat a large skillet with oil and, one at a time, brown the chicken bombs in batches.

**5.** Remove from skillet and drain on paper towels. Pour desired basting sauce into the pan and simmer for 2 to 3 minutes. Remove from heat and serve.

## Nutrition:

Energy (calories): 566 kcal

Protein: 23.47 g

Fat: 36.74 g

Carbohydrates: 41.75 g

# 289. GRILL-FRIED BUTTERMILK CHICKEN WITH PEPPERCORN GRAVY

|  |  |  |
|---|---|---|
| Preparation Time: 10 minutes | Cooking Time: 30 minutes | Servings: 8 |

## Ingredients:

**2** pounds bone-in chicken pieces

**2½** cups buttermilk

**One-half** teaspoon salt

**1** teaspoon coarse ground black pepper

**1** teaspoon dried oregano

**1** teaspoon dried thyme

**1** teaspoon smoked paprika

**One-half** teaspoon cayenne powder

**One-fourth** cup mayonnaise

**3** cloves garlic, crushed and minced

**One-fourth** cup fresh parsley, chopped

**3** cups crushed butter crackers

**Gravy**

**One-fourth** cup butter

**One-fourth** cup flour

**1** tablespoon coarse ground black pepper

**1** teaspoon salt

**½** teaspoon onion powder

**½** teaspoon garlic powder

**2½** cups milk

## Directions:

**1.** Preheat oven to 425 degrees Fahrenheit. In a skillet, heat half of the butter on the grill over medium heat.

**2.** Plate chicken in a bowl and pour buttermilk over it; add salt, pepper, oregano, thyme, paprika, and cayenne. Mix well.

**3.** Skewer the chicken on to the skewers. Cover the skewers with foil and bake in a baking sheet for 10 minutes. Take the chicken out, flip over, and bake for another 10 minutes.

**4.** Take the chicken out.

**5.** In the same skillet that the chicken was cooked in, set in the remaining butter. Stir in flour. When it is bubbling, slowly whisk in the milk, pepper, salt, onion powder, and garlic powder. Whisk continuously until the gravy thickens and is bubbling.

**6.** Add mayonnaise, parsley, and garlic. Pour over chicken.

**7.** Crush the crackers in a bowl and transfer to a separate bowl that has been linked with a baking sheet. Place a skewer, chicken, and gravy in the bowl. Cover it with butter crackers and bake for another 5 minutes. After it is done, it will be golden-brown.

**8.** Enjoy your dish!

## Nutrition:

Energy (calories): 908 kcal

Protein: 29.87 g

Fat: 83.54 g

Carbohydrates: 11.67 g

CPSIA information can be obtained
at www.ICGtesting.com
Printed in the USA
BVHW090212210421
605389BV00007B/1937

9 781802 122855